DEPARTMENT OF HEALTH

The Children Act Guidance and Regulations

Volume 6

Children with Disabilities

A NEW FRAMEWORK FOR THE CARE
AND UPBRINGING OF CHILDREN

LONDON: HMSO

© Crown copyright 1991
Applications for reproduction should be made to HMSO's Copyright Unit
First published 1991
Third impression 1995
ISBN 0 11 32145 9

Complementary titles also available from HMSO include:

The Children Act Volume 1	Court Orders ISBN 0 11 321371 9
The Children Act Volume 2	Family Support, Day care and Educational Provision for Young Children ISBN 0 11 321372 7
The Children Act Volume 3	Family Placements ISBN 0 11 321375 1
The Children Act Volume 4	Residential Care ISBN 0 11 321430 8
The Children Act Volume 5	Independent Schools ISBN 0 11 321373 5
The Children Act Volume 7	Guardians Ad Litem and other Court Related Issues ISBN 0 11 321471 5
The Children Act Volume 8	Private Fostering and Miscellaneous ISBN 0 11 321473 1
The Children Act Volume 9	Adoption Issues ISBN 0 11 321473 1
The Children Act Volume 10	Index 0 11 321538 X

The Challenge of Partnership in Child Protection: Practice Guide
published January 1995, ISBN 0 11 321825 7

Preface

The guidance in this volume is issued under section 7 of the Local Authority Social Services Act 1970. It is one in a series designed to bring to managers and practitioners an understanding of the principles of the Children Act and associated regulations, to identify areas of change and to discuss the implications for policies, procedures and practice. It is not intended that any one volume should be read as a discrete entity. The Children Act was conceived as a cohesive legal framework for the care and protection of children. Each volume of guidance should therefore be read in conjunction with the others in the series and cross-references are made where appropriate. The Act emphasises sound practice and multi-agency, multi-disciplinary co-operation as described in **Working Together** and the **Principles and Practice Guide**.

The following abbreviations are used in the text where appropriate:

Social Services Department – SSD
Local Education Authority – LEA
District Health Authority – DHA

The guidance uses the masculine terms "he" and "his" to include the feminine to reflect the legislation.

Contents

CHAPTER 1 INTRODUCTION

1.1. The Children Act 1989, brings together most public and private law relating to children and establishes a new approach in England and Wales to SSD services for children and their families. This guidance considers the implications of the Act's drawing together the SSD's functions towards children which existed under the Child Care Act 1980, the National Assistance Act 1948 and Schedule 8 of the National Health Service Act 1977 so that apart from the Chronically Sick and Disabled Persons Act 1971 and the Disabled Persons (Services, Consultation and Representation) Act 1986, the SSD's functions in respect of children with disabilities are covered by the Children Act.

1.2. The Children Act provides a legal framework for a new approach to provision of services to a child with disabilities. Unification of all legislation governing the SSD's provision of services to children seeks to ensure integration of provision of services for children and requires that they must offer children with disabilities looked after by them or by other agencies, the benefit of those powers and duties which they have in respect of all children whom they look after. As with other parts of the Act, provisions in relation to children with disabilities do not stand alone but must be considered within the context of the wider range of provisions under the Act. This separate guidance does not contain any regulations or present requirements that are not contained within the other volumes in the Children Act series. Brief summaries and explanations in the context of working with children with disabilities are provided in this document to make clear the new approach to working with children with disabilities that the Act requires. This is to help local authorities (SSDs and LEAs) and the health service to consider afresh their policies and strategies for the provision of services to children with disabilities.

1.3. The Act provides new safeguards for children with disabilities which they were unable to enjoy previously unless they were in the care of the SSD (as health and welfare legislation generally made no provision for the welfare of individual children provided with services by a SSD). Requirements such as having to review the case of a child who has been living away from home, having to give consideration to his welfare and to consult him and his parents before decisions are taken, therefore, apply to children with disabilities as well as other children in need. This is without any loss of any special provisions that applied to children with disabilities prior to implementation of the Children Act.

1.4. The Children Act contains specific provisions in respect of services to children with disabilities:

- Section 23(8) requires that "where a local authority provide accommodation for a child whom they are looking after and who is disabled, they shall, so far as is reasonably practicable, secure that the accommodation is not unsuitable to his particular needs" (see Chapter 11);

- Schedule 2, paragraph 2 separates out the requirement on local authorities to open and maintain a register of children with disabilities in their area (see Chapter 4);

- Schedule 2, paragraph 3 provides that a local authority may assess a child's needs for the purpose of the Children Act at the same time as any assessment under certain other Acts (see Chapter 5);

- Schedule 2, paragraph 9 requires local authorities to provide services for children with disabilities which are designed to minimise the effects of the children's disabilities and to give them the opportunity to lead lives that are as normal as possible (see Chapter 6).

1.5. SSDs have a clear, positive and separate duty to provide services to children with disabilities in their area. SSDs developing policies for children with disabilities within the overall framework of the Children Act should ensure that they have a specific policy on integration of their services which meets their general duties and powers towards children and families under the Children Act. Policies should take account of the wishes and views of the local community including user groups. Every effort should be made to work collaboratively in team and multi-agency structures in order to avoid the creation of separate and segregated services.

1.6. Work with children with disabilities in the context of the Children Act should be based on the following principles:

- The welfare of the child should be safeguarded and promoted by those providing services;
- A primary aim should be to promote access for all children to the same range of services;
- Children with disabilities are children first;
- Recognition of the importance of parents and families in children's lives;
- Partnership between parents and local authorities and other agencies; and
- The views of children and parents should be sought and taken into account.

1.7. In support of these principles, the Act:

- Provides for parents to retain parental responsibility for their children (even when there is a court order committing children to care);
- Imposes new duties on the SSD towards children *in need* and their families. The definition of children *in need* includes children with disabilities;
- Requires SSDs to provide services designed to minimise the effect of a child's disabilities and to give a child with disabilities the opportunity to lead as normal a life as possible.
- Requires SSDs providing services to give due consideration to the child's religious persuasion, racial origin, cultural and linguistic background;
- Provides for a collaborative and inter-agency approach in the provision of services to families and children;
- Gives SSDs new responsibilities for children it is looking after; and
- Provides a range of new court orders to protect children at risk.

1.8. Treating children as children first is of paramount importance. However, there is a need for all staff who may be involved in providing a service to a child with disabilities to be aware of legislation and local arrangements with specific relevance to the provision of services for people with disabilities. Work with many children with disabilities requires particular experience and expertise and SSDs should ensure arrangements provide for the necessary advice, expertise and resources to be available to their staff when needed. The Children Act provides that assessment arrangements for children who may be in need can be carried out simultaneously with assessments under the Chronically Sick and Disabled Persons Act 1970, the Education Act 1981, the Disabled Persons Act 1986 or any other enactment (see Chapter 5). SSDs should discuss with LEAs, DHAs (and where appropriate NHS Trusts) arrangements for joint assessment in appropriate cases and the provision of health services under the collaborative arrangements in the light of the Children Act and the NHS reforms.

CHAPTER 2 PARENTAL RESPONSIBILITY

2.1. The Act introduces a new concept of *parental responsibility*. 'Parental responsibility' is defined to include all the rights, powers, authority and duties of parents in relation to a child and his property (section 3(1)). The term parental responsibility unifies the many references in legislation to parental rights, powers, authority and duties. An understanding and acceptance of parental responsibility as a continuing responsibility, whatever the circumstances of the child (other than in adoption), is essential in working with families in the spirit of the Act.

WHO HAS PARENTAL RESPONSIBILITY?

2.2. Where a child's parents were or have been married to each other at or after the time of his conception, they each have parental responsibility for him (section 2(1), as extended by section 1 of the Family Law Reform Act 1987, section 2(3)). Otherwise, the mother alone has parental responsibility unless the father acquires it by a court order or an agreement under the Act (section 2(2)).

2.3. The father who does not have parental responsibility may acquire it in one of two ways:

(a) with the mother, he may make 'a parental responsibility agreement'; or

(b) he may apply to court for an order which gives him parental responsibility (section 4(1)).

2.4. A parental responsibility agreement was not available under the old law (although a parent could make an agreement about the exercise of her parental rights and duties under section 1(2) of the Guardianship Act 1973). It is intended as a simple method by which unmarried parents may share parental responsibility without going to court and will have to be officially recorded in the prescribed manner (section 4(2)). The effect of a parental responsibility agreement is the same as a court order conferring parental responsibility. Both may only be brought to an end by a court order on the application of a person with parental responsibility for the child or (with the leave of the court) of the child himself, if he has sufficient understanding to make the application (section 4(3) and (4)).

2.5. A court order which gives a father parental responsibility is similar to an order to give him parental rights and duties under section 4 of the Family Law Reform Act 1987. (An order under the 1987 Act which was in force at the commencement of the Children Act is deemed to be an order under section 4 of the latter statute: Schedule 14, paragraph 4). Where a residence order is made in favour of a father (section 12(1)) an order under section 4 of the Children Act must be made. This is to ensure that a father who is entitled to have the child live with him under a court order will always have parental responsibility for him. If that residence order is later discharged, the parental responsibility order will not come to an end unless the court specifically decides that it should (section 12(4)). A father who does not have parental responsibility is still a parent for the purpose of the Act.

WHO ELSE MAY ACQUIRE PARENTAL RESPONSIBILITY?

2.6. People other than parents may acquire parental responsibility by appointment as a guardian or by an order of the court (a residence order or an emergency protection order). SSDs may acquire it by a care order or an emergency protection order.

THE EXERCISE OF PARENTAL RESPONSIBILITY

2.7. The fact that one person acquires parental responsibility does not in itself remove another's parental responsibility (section 2(6)). After separation or divorce, parents retain their parental responsibility. Existing orders regarding custody, care and control and access continue to have effect after the Act comes into force. The fact that a person has parental responsibility for a child under the Act does not however mean that he may act incompatibly with an existing order (section 2(8) and Schedule 14, paragraphs 6(3) and 7(3)).

2.8. Parental responsibility for a child cannot be passed on to someone else or otherwise be given up (section 2(9)). However, where a person acquired parental responsibility under a court order (or parental responsibility agreement or by appointment as guardian), the court may later bring that order (or agreement or appointment) to an end.

2.9. A person with parental responsibility may arrange for another person to meet that responsibility on his behalf (section 2(9)). Such an arrangement might be useful while a person with parental responsibility is unable to act, perhaps due to a stay in hospital or a trip abroad. It does not affect any liability of the person with parental responsibility which follows from a failure to meet his parental responsibility (section 2(11)).

2.10. Where more than one person has parental responsibility for a child at the same time, one may act independently of the other or others to meet that responsibility (section 2(5) and (7)). Unlike earlier legislation, the Act does not attempt to impose a duty on one parent to consult the other or to give one a right of veto against the action of the other. If necessary, one person with parental responsibility may ask a court to make a specific issue order or condition in a residence order which would require the other to inform him before a particular step is taken or not taken (section 8 and 11(7)(b)). The onus of applying to court will not generally fall on the person who is caring for the child. This person will therefore be able to respond to circumstances as they arise.

WHEN A CHILD IS IN CARE

2.11. The only exception to the rule which permits independent action to meet shared parental responsibility arises when a child is in care. Here, the SSD is given power to determine the extent to which another person with parental responsibility may act (section 33(3)(b) and (4)).

2.12. The concept of partnership between SSDs and parents reflects the importance of the family in children's lives and that the best place for the child to be brought up is usually in his own home. This is as important in relation to children subject to care orders as for those who may be accommodated by the SSD by a voluntary arrangement. For a fuller explanation of parental responsibility and relevant legislation see Volume 2 in this series.

CARE BUT NOT PARENTAL RESPONSIBILITY

2.13. If a person has care of a child for whom he does not have parental responsibility, section 3(5) of the Act empowers him to do what is reasonable in all the circumstances to safeguard or promote the child's welfare. This is the person who in old terminology had 'actual custody' of the child. Of course, such a person may not act in a way which conflicts with the Act, in particular with an order under it, except in the limited circumstances in which he may be required to act to protect the child from danger.

CHAPTER 3 CHILDREN IN NEED

DEFINITION

3.1. The Act defines a category of children *in need* for whom the SSD should provide services, if necessary, to safeguard and promote their welfare. A child is defined by the Act as being *in need* if:

'(a) he is unlikely to achieve or maintain, or to have the opportunity of achieving or maintaining, a reasonable standard of health or development without the provision for him of services by a local authority under this Part [of the Act];

(b) his health or development is likely to be significantly impaired, or further impaired, without the provision for him of such services; or

(c) he is disabled.'

'"development" means physical, intellectual, emotional, social or behavioural development', and

'"health" means physical or mental health'.

3.2. The Children Act mirrors the National Assistance Act 1948 definition of disability, stating that:

'a child is disabled if he is blind, deaf or dumb or suffers from mental disorder of any kind or is substantially and permanently handicapped by illness, injury or congenital deformity or such other disability as may be prescribed'.

Thus a person with a disability qualifies for services before and after the age of 18.

GENERAL DUTY TO PROVIDE SERVICES

3.3. The Act's definitions of in need and disability provide the basis of a general duty on the SSD to provide an appropriate range and level of services to safeguard and promote the welfare of children in need and '*so far as is consistent with that duty to promote the upbringing of such children by their families*'. This general duty is supported by other specific duties and powers such as facilitation of 'the provision by others, including in particular voluntary organisations of services' (section 17(5) and Schedule 2). These provisions encourage SSDs to provide day and domiciliary services, guidance and counselling, respite care and a range of other services as a means of supporting children in need (including children with disabilities) within their families. The Act recognises that sometimes a child can only be helped by providing services for other members of his family (section 17(3)) 'if it [the service] is provided with a view to safeguarding or promoting the child's welfare'. 'Family' in relation to such a child, includes any person who has parental responsibility for the child and any other person with whom he has been living. The SSD may make such arrangements as they see fit for *any* person to provide services and support 'may include giving assistance in kind, or in exceptional circumstances in cash' (section 17(6)). However, where it is the SSD's view that a child's welfare is adequately provided for and no unmet need exists, they need not act. SSDs now have a general duty to provide day care services and supervise activities for children in need aged five and under and not at school and for school age children outside school hours and in school holidays. Children have common needs in terms of care, affection and a stimulating environment in which to develop. The Children Act's definition of children in need and the range of duties and powers provided in Part III of the

Act should therefore be seen as an important opportunity not only to ensure that children with disabilities are treated as children first, but also to ensure access to the range of generic and specialist provision available to support children and families in their own homes and their local communities.

3.4. The SSD is not obliged to provide all the services which may be needed itself. Section 17(5)(a) of the Act states that every SSD shall facilitate the provision by others (including in particular voluntary organisations) of services which the local authority have power to provide by virtue of this section or sections 18, 20, 23 and 24 of the Act. SSDs may also arrange for others to provide services on their behalf (section 17(5)(b)).

3.5. In deciding which services are needed by individual families, SSDs will need to give careful attention not only to families' stated preferences but to the contribution which other statutory and voluntary agencies might make. The potential contributions of the respective agencies in the statutory, voluntary and independent sectors are shown in Annex A. Coordinating packages of services from multiple service providers will require time and resources and the compatibility of services offered should be carefully assessed. Individual children and families will have very different levels of need which may fluctuate throughout the year according to other pressures of family life. The provision of education, respite care and day care will not be effective unless they are tailored to the needs of the child and family. Arrangements must be such that parents are reassured that the child will receive good quality care and that the child's interests are met. In some instances provision of a discrete service (eg aids and adaptations to a house or transport in order to use a local after school club) may assist the child and his family to lead fulfilling lives without other service provision.

IDENTIFICATION OF NEED AND PUBLICISING SERVICES

3.6. Paragraph 1 of Schedule 2 to the Act requires SSDs to identify the extent to which there are children in need in their area and to publicise the availability of services. SSDs should build on existing links with community groups, voluntary organisations and ethnic minority groups to involve them in planning services and as a sounding board when formulating policies. The publicity required must include information about services provided both by the SSD and, to the extent they consider it appropriate, about such provision by others (eg voluntary organisations). Publicity should be clearly presented and accessible to all groups in the community, taking account of linguistic and cultural factors and the needs of people with communication difficulties. SSDs should take reasonable steps to ensure that all those who might benefit from such services receive the relevant information.

CHAPTER 4 CO-ORDINATING SERVICES

COLLABORATIVE WORKING

4.1. New organisational links between SSDs and NHS staff will need to be developed if they are to implement the Act. DHAs may help SSDs to fulfil their duty to take reasonable steps to identify the extent to which there are children in need in their area by identifying the numbers and needs of children in their areas who are disabled through physical, sensory or learning disablement, mental disorders and chronic illness. Such assistance would not require identification of individual children. In respect of an individual child SSDs will need to consider in co-operation with other relevant agencies such as DHAs or LEAs, a child's overall developmental needs – physical, social, intellectual, emotional and behavioural in assessing what sort of services are required. The Children Act requires SSDs, LEAs, local housing authorities, DHAs and NHS Trusts to comply with a request from a SSD for assistance in providing services under Part III of the Act so long as it is compatible with their own legal duty or other duties and does not unduly prejudice the discharge of any of their functions (section 27).

REGISTER OF CHILDREN WITH DISABILITIES

4.2. The Act replaces and separates out the previous requirement placed on SSDs to keep registers of children with disabilities in their area. Paragraph 2 of Schedule 2 to the Children Act requires SSDs to keep a register of children with disabilities. This provision, which is designed to help their service planning and monitoring, originated from directions made under the National Assistance Act 1948 in relation to disabled persons. There is no corresponding duty on parents to agree to registration (which is a voluntary procedure) and services are not dependant on registration. Registration can contribute positively to coherent planning of service provision for children with disabilities under the Children Act. However, registration will necessitate clear criteria for definitions of disability. This will be decided best in discussions between SSDs, LEAs and DHAs. As will the fact that registers should be regularly updated.

4.3. SSDs whilst acknowledging the legal definition of disability in the Children Act, will need to liaise with their education and health counterparts to achieve an understanding of disability which permits early identification; which facilitates joint working; which encourages parents to agree to registration and which is meaningful in terms of planning services for the child in question and children in general. The creation of a joint register of children with disabilities between health, education and social services would greatly facilitate collaboration in identification and a co-ordinated provision of services under the Act. It is possible for a SSD to arrange for another agency (a DHA for example) to maintain and operate the register on their behalf. In such circumstances responsibility for the register remains with the SSD.

4.4. Whichever agency is the first to identify a child having a disability whether it is the LEA, SSD or child health services they should initiate discussions with the parents about services or procedures which might be beneficial to the child and family. This should include an explanation of what other agencies can provide and information about the register. The registration of children with disabilities will be effective and productive only if parents and children are regarded as partners in the assessment process and as experts in their own right, from whom professionals may have much to learn. Parents and children are likely to be less anxious about the registration process if they are given clear and comprehensible information in accessible formats about the purpose and use of the register and if they contribute directly to what is recorded about their child's special needs. It should be made clear that the register has no connection with child protection registers and that child protection registration is an entirely separate process. In making use of the register SSDs should ensure that confidentiality about individual children and families is maintained. The Department issued a circular (LAC(88)17) in September 1988 containing guidance on the safeguarding and disclosure of personal information held in SSD records. If the register is computerised, the provisions of the Data Protection Act 1987 will apply.

4.5. Decisions about registration should not be made when an older child or parents are still in a time of considerable emotional stress at the identification of the child's potential disability or special need. The child's and parents' need for support should be the first consideration. Any sense of grief and loss at this time should be acknowledged. Counselling provided should be sensitive to individual racial, cultural, linguistic, religious needs or communication difficulties. Discussion of registration should take place at a later date.

CHAPTER 5 ASSESSMENT AND PLANNING PROCESS

5.1. SSDs will need to develop clear assessment procedures for children in need within agreed criteria which take account of the child's and family's needs and preferences, racial and ethnic origins, their culture, religion and any special needs relating to the circumstances of individual families. The assessment procedures are not laid down in primary legislation or regulations, but assessments under the Children Act should be undertaken in the context of Part 3 and Schedule 2 of the Act (as part of the process of recognition of need and the identification of appropriate services). The Children Act empowers SSDs to combine assessments under the Children Act with those under other legislation such as the Education Act 1981; the Disabled Persons Act 1986 and the Chronically Sick and Disabled Persons Act 1970 (paragraph 3 of Schedule 2 to the Children Act). Formal assessment under the Education Act 1981 already involves collaboration between DHAs, LEAs and SSDs and parents. The procedures under the Education Act 1981 are likely to contribute significantly to assessment by SSDs and can be used as a basis for further collaborative decision-making about the wider needs of children and families. The Disabled Persons Act 1986 requires SSDs to assess young people with disabilities at the time they leave school for a range of welfare services as outlined in the Chronically Sick and Disabled Persons Act 1970. At eighteen years of age, young persons who have a continuing need for community care services, or who may require them for the first time, are covered by the provisions of the NHS and Community Care Act 1990, which include an assessment of their need for services.

5.2. In many cases children with disabilities will need continuing services throughout their lives. It will therefore be particularly important that for these children, the assessment process takes a longer perspective than is usual or necessary for children without disabilities, who will usually cease to have a need for services after reaching adulthood.

5.3 The requirements of children with disabilities may need to be met from a number of sources. In conducting assessments and managing the care provided, SSDs will need to ensure that all necessary expertise is marshalled and that all those providing services are involved from both within and beyond the SSD. The outcome of assessment should be a holistic and realistic picture of the individual and family being assessed, which takes into account their strengths and capacities as well as any difficulties and which acknowledges the need to make provision appropriate to the family's cultural background and their expressed views and preferences.

5.4. The SSD's provision of services to children with disabilities should involve an initial assessment of need, a continuing process of reassessment and review of the plan for the child. Continuity should not be broken for reasons which concern organisational or administrative convenience rather than the welfare of the child or young person. A smooth transition, when the young person reaches 18 and comes within the provisions of the NHS and Community Care Act 1990 should be the objective.

NHS AND COMMUNITY CARE ACT 1990 – CARE MANAGEMENT

5.5. In the White Paper **'Caring for People'** and subsequent policy guidance issued in November 1990, care management and assessment are key processes in the provision of community care services. This has relevance for

SSDs in planning services for children under the Children Act and may provide a useful model for consideration.

5.6. The NHS and Community Care Act 1990 requires the SSD to assess the needs of persons who may require community care services. If during the course of assessment it appears that a person is disabled, the SSD is required if requested to decide upon the need for services under Section 4 of the Disabled Persons Act 1986. Over time, these assessment arrangements will be expected to form part of wider care management systems that cover all arrangements for the care of the service user from the beginning to the end of their contact with the SSD.

5.7. Policy guidance **(Caring for People: Community Care in the Next Decade and Beyond – Policy Guidance: Chapter 3 – Care Management and Assessment)** describes 3 distinct processes which characterise care management in its most comprehensive form:

'– assessment of the users' circumstances

– design of a 'care package' in agreement with users' carers and relevant agencies to meet the identified needs within the care resources available, including help from willing and able carers

– implementation and monitoring of the agreed package: review of the outcomes for users and carers; and any necessary revision of service provision.'

5.8. An important feature of the care management process is that it is based on a needs-led approach within resource availability. Responsibility for assessment and care planning should be progressively separated from service provision in order to focus on needs, where possible having the tasks carried out by different staff. The intention is to ensure that people are not fitted into existing services, but that services are adapted to individual needs. This separation enables discrepancies between assessed needs and available service to be identified.

5.9. Care management arrangements also take account of the multiple service providers which will be required to meet the majority of special needs. The approach aims to encourage the identification of the full range of services which may be needed. The SSD will have overall responsibility for the co-ordination of the services required. However, the day to day management and provision of these services may rest elsewhere. Packages of support can be put together using the statutory and the voluntary and independent sectors thereby making use of whatever pattern of provision has been developed within the context of a particular SSD.

CHILD CARE PRACTICE

5.10. Good child care practice incorporates many of the features of care management. The procedures of the Education Act 1981, for example, encourage the resolution of a child's special educational needs where necessary by the definition of an educational care package which includes services from the child health service, SSD and the LEA concerned. Some SSDs are now developing 'packages of support' for children.

5.11. There is a further similarity between child care practice and care management in that the aim is normally to provide one worker with continuing responsibility for providing and co-ordinating services. This is one means by which care management may be delivered, and may be the means best suited to meet the needs of children with disabilities. It should be emphasised, however, that the appointment of a single care manager is but one way of delivering care management, the responsibility for different aspects of which may be shared by different workers. Moreover it should be emphasised that where responsibility is given to a single care manager, that care manager should be from the agency most relevant to the current needs of the child with a disability, and that this agency may change over time.

5.12. The distinction between the terms 'key worker' and 'care manager' should also be noted. The range of responsibilities carried by care managers and the fact that they are not involved in direct service delivery distinguishes their role from that of key workers.

5.13. Standards of service are agreed between the SSD and service providers and the individual package of care may reflect a very wide diversity of service provision. The parents and children concerned are important contributors to the planning process. But the development of a flexible child care service for children with disabilities will not be possible without the closest liaison between health, education and social services and the use of whatever team approach to special needs is available in the locality. If district handicap, child development or community mental handicap teams are to contribute positively to assessment and planning services to children with disabilities (and to forward planning under the NHS and Community Care Act when the young person makes the transition to adult services), SSD representation on and involvement in the work of the team in question will be crucial. Ensuring an input from a SSD representative into existing teams will often be a cost-effective way of enabling all local resources to be used in the most effective way. Additionally the representative in question will have direct access to team members and to the planning processes of the other services.

THE MANAGEMENT PROCESS

5.14. Many children with disabilities will require support from a very wide range of services. Their need for services will often be a continuing need. An on going process of assessment, monitoring and review will therefore be essential in order to ensure appropriateness and effectiveness of service provision. Where a multi-disciplinary team already exists, the appointment of key workers or care manager may pose no problems. Since the development of individual packages of care will necessitate negotiations with service managers and budget holders across a range of agencies, a team base for such an arrangement may be the most effective. But care management will require skilled support, training and regular appraisal. In implementing the new arrangements for children with disabilities under the Children Act, SSDs will need to look carefully at:

- the range of existing assessment arrangements within agencies providing services for children with disabilities within the SSD in question;
- the recording and monitoring systems to be used by the SSD in assessing and planning to meet needs;
- the use of the register with regard to recording and reviewing provision;
- the extent to which existing multi-disciplinary teams can be utilised and developed in creating shared assessment systems;
- how best to involve consumers – parents and children – in the assessment process and to ensure that they have ownership of the outcomes of any assessment process; and
- procedures when the young person reaches the age of 18 and the provisions of the NHS and Community Care Act 1990 and the Children Act 1989 overlap. The aim must be to ensure by early planning that a seamless transition to adult services takes place.

5.15. Policy guidance requires that where community care arrangements are fully implemented SSDs will need to have available published information accessible to all potential service users and carers, including those with any communication difficulty or difference in language or culture. The information should set out the types of community care available, the criteria for provision of services, the assessment procedures to agree needs and ways of addressing them and the standards by which the care management system (including assessment) will be measured.

5.16. SSDs should include in this information care management and assessment arrangements for children with disabilities. Such information could be linked to wider duties to provide information on the full range of local services and could be made available to children and families undergoing assessment through procedures relating to the 1981 Act and other relevant legislation.

5.17. Detailed practice guidance has been prepared by the Department's Social Services Inspectorate on the implementation of care management and assessment arrangements. Many of the principles are also applicable to aspects of child care. SSDs should refer to the community care assessment and care management practice guide.

CHAPTER 6 PLANNING OF SERVICES IN PARTNERSHIP WITH PARENTS AND CHILDREN

6.1. A key theme in the Children Act is that of partnership with parents and, where the child is of sufficient understanding with the child. The concept of partnership is not new, but is based on well established beliefs that:

● the family home is the natural and most appropriate place for the majority of children;

● families are already caring for children, and supporting them to do so is, in most cases, in the best interests of the child and best allocation of resources in the SSD;

● children are individuals with their own needs, wishes and feelings;

● the family has a unique and special knowledge of a child and can therefore contribute significantly to that child's health and development – albeit often in partnership with a range of service providers; and

● families provide continuity for children throughout their childhood – and, in the context of the Children Act, families are recognised as being more widely defined than parents and brothers and sisters and other relatives, and often play an important part in the life of a child.

6.2. Parents and children from all backgrounds, ethnic origins and different lifestyles, will need clear information and sensitive responses when they seek support. The services needed may be day care; health services and educational provision which all parents and children will use sometime or a targeted service to meet a particular need.

6.3. The Arrangements for Placement of Children (General) Regulations 1991 and the Review of Children Case's Regulations 1991 together with specific placement regulations are the framework for the provision of the service of accommodation to children looked after by SSDs or accommodated by voluntary organisations or in registered children's homes (see Chapter 11). Good practice requires that the same approach is taken to the provision of services other than accommodation. This is implicit in the provision contained in paragraph 6 of Schedule 2 to the Act which requires that:

'every local authority shall provide services designed –

(a) to minimise the effect on disabled children within their area of their disabilities; and

(b) to give such children the opportunity to lead lives which are as normal as possible.'

PLANNING A SERVICE FOR THE INDIVIDUAL CHILD

6.4. Once a need has been identified a plan for the best service provision will be required. This may amount to no more than matching the need with an existing service in the community. Where the SSD has to allocate resources to arrange a service – for example, a family aide for the family or a day nursery place for the child – the plan should estimate how long the service may be required, what the objective of the service should be and what else others are expected to do. In order to be effective this plan should form the basis of an agreement with the child, parent or other carer and be reviewed at appropriate intervals. In planning for the individual child, the SSD should take account of the particular needs of the child – that is in relation to health, development, disability, education, religious persuasion, racial origin, gender, cultural and linguistic background, the degree (if any) to which these needs are being met by existing services to the family or child and which agencies' services are best suited to the child's needs. The needs of brothers and sisters should not be overlooked and they should be provided for as part of a package of services for the child with a disability. They may however be in need in their own right and require separate assessment. SSDs must be sensitive to the needs and requirements of ethnic minority families, and in particular ensure assessments take into account individual circumstances and are not based on a stereotypical view of what may be required. Equally partnership and consultation with parents and children on the basis of careful joint planning and agreement is the guiding principle for the provision of services whether within the family home or where children are provided with accommodation under voluntary arrangements. Such arrangements are intended to assist the parent and enhance, not undermine, the parent's authority and control. This approach should also be developed when a child is in care, provided that it does not jeopardise his welfare.

6.5. Where a child is looked after (accommodated) by the SSD, the Act requires that his views should be sought subject to his understanding (see sections 22(4)(a) and (5), 61 and 64 of the Children Act). It is required that the child's views as expressed be discussed, recorded and given due consideration when plans for the welfare of the child are in hand, before a placement decision is made and at every review meeting and at case conferences.

LISTENING TO CHILDREN

6.6. The Children Act places new duties on SSDs with regard to involving children in planning their futures. These arrangements apply whether or not the child has a disability or special need. There is a fine balance between giving children a voice and encouraging them to make informed decisions – and over-burdening them with decision-making procedures where they have insufficient experience and knowledge to make an appropriate judgement without additional support. Learning to make well-informed choices and making some mistakes should be part of every child's experience. Children and young people should be given the chance to exercise choice and their views should be taken seriously if they are unhappy about the arrangements made for them. Plans should be explained, discussed and if necessary, reassessed in the light of the child's views. The social worker should be aware and acknowledge that there may be good reasons why the child's views are different from those of his parents or the SSD. The more mature the child, the more fully he will be able to enter into discussion about plans and proposals and participate in the decision-making process. When older children are involved, and particularly in a case of self-referral, there may well be a different perception of the child's needs and interests as seen by the child and his parents. With young children, the social worker should make efforts to communicate with the child and discover his real feelings. All children need to be given information and appropriate explanations so that they are in a position to develop views and make choices. They should also have access to the representations procedure (see Chapter 14).

SUFFICIENT UNDERSTANDING

6.7. If the child has complex needs or communication difficulties arrangements must be made to establish his views. Decisions may be made incorrectly about children with disabilities because of ignorance about the true implications of the disability and the child's potential for growth and development. Children with disabilities have the same rights as other children and adults to have access to information held about them in social services and health service records. Their ability to give consent or refusal to any action including examination, assessment or treatment is only limited by the general conditions regarding sufficient understanding which apply to other children under the Children Act. However, sufficient understanding may be misunderstood. Even children with severe learning disabilities or very limited expressive language can communicate preferences if they are asked in the right way by people who understand their needs and have the relevant skills to listen to them. No assumptions should be made about 'categories' of children with disabilities who cannot share in decision-making or give consent to or refuse examination, assessment or treatment.

6.8. Consulting children with disabilities requires expertise and staff may need special training. In the case of a child (or a parent) with communication difficulties provision of a sign language interpreter, large print, tape and braille may need to be made if communication is to be effective. The need for an interpreter should be considered where the family's first language is not English. For children with no verbal communication, information technology aids should be used. Necessary experience and expertise should be provided for in staffing of services and through relationships with other professions and services and with the community. Such training might usefully be linked to existing training on equal opportunities and anti-discrimination.

PARTICIPATION

6.9. Participation will be a token exercise unless careful consideration is given to supporting and informing children and parents about the consequences of any decision being taken – and about the options which they need to consider in making a preference. Only a clear and consistent policy of involvement of children and parents during assessment, at decision-making meetings and in case reviews and conferences from this early stage will avoid conflicts and adversarial debates. Participation by parents and children will be limited if they do not have adequate information or if the professional agencies concerned are not aware of relevant sources of information. Parent-held health records presuppose eventual transfer from parents to their older children. Many schools operate records of achievement, which provide statements of positive achievements in social as well as educational areas. Children who are looked after may have Lifestory books and other documentation about their lives and preferences.

CHAPTER 7 <u>WORKING WITH THE COMMUNITY</u>

7.1. The Children Act requires SSDs to provide services to support families in bringing up children in need. SSDs are also required to facilitate the provision of such services by others, including in particular, voluntary organisations. The Children Act requires SSDs to facilitate the provision of family support services, day care, accommodation and after care by others and to publicise such services provided by others (section 17(5) and paragraph 1(2) of Schedule 2). Family support will require effective coordination, communication and mutual respect between and with professionals and services in the community. It will also necessitate sensitive assessment of parents' and children's preferences in terms of family support and require providing them with full information in order that they can make an informed choice. Some families caring for children with complex or multiple disabilities may have neither the time nor the energy to contribute to assessment and planning unless they are given personal counselling, support and representation. Working with the child and family in the family home may also contribute to realistic assessment of overall needs and preferences and contribute to a realistic partnership in assessment.

7.2. SSDs have a duty to inform parents of the local range of services which can support families with children in need at home. Voluntary organisations, as well as the education service, may provide a range of provision which is flexible and can be adapted to individual family needs. A number of local authorities now work with the voluntary sector in providing advice. However, the OPCS Reports (1989) noted that most parents did not know of relevant local voluntary organisations. All statutory and voluntary services should ensure that information is given to parents.

THE VOLUNTARY SECTOR

7.3. The voluntary sector has always been a rich and creative resource for consumer groups in the United Kingdom. There are many local and national voluntary organisations in the UK concerned with disability and most have local groups and increasingly collaborate with other organisations in the wider voluntary sector. Apart from providing personal support for parents, they offer a range of practical services ranging from loans of equipment and holiday playschemes to residential or education services. All provide information and most offer counselling and advice.

7.4. Voluntary organisations are not only concerned with the important area of consumer support. Many have pioneered new ways of working with children with complex needs and from minority groups, for example those with multiple disabilities or challenging behaviour. Voluntary organisations, like their local authority counterparts, cannot provide services in a vacuum. As they become part of the wider network of provision used by SSDs clear policies for their inclusion in *planning* local services – as well as arrangements for accountability and procedures such as complaints – will be essential. They need access to advice from a range of professionals, including psychologists, social workers, therapists, and the education service. The use of voluntary agencies for direct service provision should, therefore, be accompanied by:

(a) Early involvement in planning services within the authority as a whole.

(b) Explicit service agreements which involve children and families and ensure access to relevant professional advice.

(c) Agreed assessment, recording and review procedures.

(d) Shared training opportunities – both as trainers and for staff working in the voluntary sector to have training opportunities with their local authority counterparts.

7.5. In some instances, the role of the voluntary agency may not be to provide specific regular services such as day or residential care, but to offer representation and advocacy for the parents and child or to develop formal representation schemes on behalf of the SSD in question. Some SSDs are already utilising their local voluntary sector to provide representation schemes or to provide support for 'hard to reach' groups of children such as those living in Travellers' families or in homeless family accommodation.

CHAPTER 8 <u>SERVICES TO CHILDREN LIVING WITH THEIR FAMILIES</u>

DOMICILIARY SERVICES

8.1. As stated in paragraph 7.1 services for children with disabilities may be appropriately provided in the home. Investing in a package of family support services to assist parents looking after a child with disabilities at home will in most cases be a better alternative than residential care. A home care service can provide valuable day to day support to families. For example, the Portage Home Teaching scheme for parents of preschool children with disabilities has demonstrated the importance of a known trained and supported home visitor making regular visits to a family in order to monitor the child's progress, to identify goals and structure simple teaching programmes in order to reach them. Portage has been a major source of skill-training for professionals as well as for parents. Health visitors, community nurses, home liaison teachers, psychologists, social workers and (in some instances) volunteers have learned how to work as a team through using Portage; how to work directly with parents and share skills and expertise and, most importantly, to be able to offer parents positive involvement with their child to help maximise the child's potential.

8.2. Portage is an important example of involving all consumers in a programme which teaches success, which is sensitive to social, personal and cultural variables, and which can be utilised in a wide range of care settings. Such partnership is not, however, an alternative to the full range of support services such as respite care, aids and equipment and appropriate housing.

8.3. Services in the home for young children with disabilities will also be provided by LEAs or DHAs. Many LEAs provide peripatetic or home liaison teachers (particularly when a child has a specific disability such as hearing or visual impairment). Health visitors have an important role in providing support on a range of issues relating to the care of young children. They also have the advantage of providing a service for all young children and their families and are seen as widely acceptable and practical advisers for any family within their locality.

8.4. There are considerable advantages to caring for a child in his own home during the absence of his parents or other carer, rather than placing the child away in residential or foster care. This might be particularly important where the family home has been adapted to suit that particular child's needs. Equivalent provision may not necessarily be available in the respite care home, and there could be positive benefits in minimising disruption to the child's normal lifestyle.

FAMILY CENTRES

8.5. Every effort should be made to enable families with young children with disabilities to use local services generally available to children and their families wherever possible. The family centres, which SSDs are now required to provide for children in their area as a community resource (paragraph 9 of Schedule 2), may provide a range of activities ranging from counselling and general support with parenting to occupational, social, cultural and recreational activities. Family Centres work with whole families can provide a base for friendship, support and access to local services. A family centre may offer opportunities for collaborative work with the LEA and child health services and act as a referral point for families seeking other services such as daycare. In addition to family centres, preschool playgroups, mother and toddler groups and local parent organisations may provide opportunities for families with a child with a disability to participate in the lives of their local community. Sometimes a family centre or play-group may need some extra help or advice from the SSD in order to help a child with special needs. Specialist advice to such family support services should therefore be part of wider SSD planning for children with disabilities and their families.

BEFRIENDING SCHEMES

8.6. In addition to services provided through statutory agencies many voluntary agencies run a range of early support and home visiting programmes. For example, volunteer befriending schemes such as those first pioneered and now supported by Home Start Consultancy provide home visitors – usually a more experienced parent who has had some training – who help parents under stress cope with young children. Volunteers provided by a local Home Start scheme also help parents use or attend other community resources such as parents/toddler groups, toy libraries and playgroups. In the case of parents with a child with disabilities a volunteer may ensure that they have opportunities to discuss the natural concerns common to all parents as well as the more specific ones relating to the child's particular disability. It is desirable to consider the need for training or information for the volunteers so that they can help the family in the most effective way. Attention should also be paid to providing support and back-up for such volunteers and the befriending scheme itself.

8.7. Many national voluntary organisations have local groups which can support parents of children with developmental delay, health problems or disabilities. Most areas also have informal self-help groups. Meeting other parents with a child with a disability may be a positive experience and can alleviate the isolation and depression which many parents acknowledge in the early years. In some instances parents may hesitate to join a special group, either because they are still coming to terms with their child's disability or because they are anxious that they or their child may not be accepted. Visits to parents at home in advance of a first meeting (or support by a friendly professional such as a health visitor, social worker or another parent) should be considered. Parents additionally should be encouraged to use Toy Libraries, Playgroups and Opportunity Groups and other local resources which will provide support and friendship in the family's own neighbourhood.

DAY CARE

8.8. Guidance on standards, quality and regulation of daycare services for young children is contained in Volume 2 of the Children Act 1989 series together with advice on the new duty to review such services every 3 years, consulting DHAs and others as part of the process and publishing a report.

8.9. The development of young children with disabilities or special educational needs is more likely to be enhanced through attending a day care service for under eights or educational service for under fives used by all children. Policy and registration officers, providers and practitioners need to consider the means whereby this aim might be achieved, in discussion with experts in the field such as health professionals and people working for relevant voluntary organisations and parents and children. In making arrangements for integrating children with disabilities with other children in a day care or pre-school setting, particular attention should be paid to the physical environment, staff/child ratios, and training (eg in sign language or alternative methods of communication for the profoundly deaf).

8.10. SSDs will wish to ensure that integration is properly addressed as part of the registration system under which they have to decide about the fitness of intending day care providers and childminders, and the suitability of the premises and equipment where the children will be cared for. This should involve finding out about intending providers' or childminders' views on caring for children with disabilities, and their understanding about what this involves.

Depending on the particular circumstances of the applicant, the local authority may wish to impose specific requirements on a person's registration so that children with disabilities receive an acceptable standard of care when they are placed in a group day care setting or with a childminder.

8.11. Some intending providers or childminders may be reluctant to take on the responsibility of caring for a child with a disability, because they are concerned about their capacity to provide adequate care. This needs to be handled sensitively, but registration officers should seek to clarify the needs of individual children and the support that will be available in appropriate cases.

8.12. In the exercise of their day care review duty (section 19) SSDs will wish to ensure that the process covers services for children with disabilities, access to them, information about them and parental involvement. The arrangements for the review should enable all those concerned about services for children with disabilities – parents, providers, health professionals and voluntary bodies – to play a full part so that their concerns are fully represented.

CHAPTER 9 WORKING WITH EDUCATION SERVICES

LEA INVOLVEMENT WITH SSDs

9.1. Joint Circular **HN(89)20/HN(FP)(89)(19)/LASSL(89)7/WOC54/89/ DES:22/89. Assessments and Statements of Special Educational Needs: Procedures within the Education, Health and Social Services** clearly acknowledges that assessment cannot be seen as a single-agency approach, whatever the specific purpose or outcome of the particular assessment procedure. Paragraph 17 of this circular notes that:

'When it is thought that a child may need special educational provision, the positive and constructive approach is to focus on his or her needs rather than on disabilities. The feelings and perceptions of the child concerned should be taken into account and older children and young persons should be able to share in discussions on their needs and any proposed provision. The extent to which a learning difficulty hinders a child's development does not depend solely on the nature and severity of that difficulty. Other significant factors include the personal resources and attributes of the child as well as the help and support provided at home and the provison made by the school and the LEA and other statutory and voluntary agencies. A child's special educational needs are thus related both to abilities and disabilities and to the nature and extent of the interaction of these with his or her environment.'

9.2. Circular 22/89 acknowledges the multifactorial nature of assessment and the extent to which a range of factors will encourage or impede a child in his or her development. LEAs are reminded that in carrying out assessments of a child's special *educational* needs, they must make clear distinctions between:

(i)   the child's relevant past and present levels of functioning, emotional states and interests and how these present resources and deficiencies in relation to the educational demands which will be made on the child;

(ii)   the analysis of the child's consequent learning difficulties;

(iii) the specification of goals for change in the child and environment (including school, home and the wider community);

(iv)   the specification of the child's requirement for different kinds of approaches, facilities or resources, in order to facilitate access to the National Curriculum, with any modifications that are considered essential;

(v)   the perceptions and wishes of the parent and child;

(vi)   the special educational provision and services required to meet the identified needs.

9.3. The LEA is also reminded that the monitoring and assessment and review of each child's progress should be seen as a continuous process. A process which begins at birth and continues in the family home and with health and social services *before* a child becomes known to the LEA. The 1981 Act, like the Children Act, clearly defines the need for communication between teachers, the school health service and SSDs as well as between the LEA and SSDs at a senior management level. Assistance before a situation becomes critical will be more effective than formal assessment procedures initiated too late and in isolation. The needs of some children will be first identified while they are living with their family. Statutory assessments under Section 5 of the 1981 Act may sometimes be required for children who are living in provision made by the local authority such as foster placements; residential care homes or whilst placed in an indepenent school for primarily residential care needs. Circular 22/89 highlights four particular cases when a SSD or health authority may initiate an assessment of a child's potential special *educational* needs or ask for the decisions reached at a previous assessment to be formally reviewed or reassessed because of concern about their appropriateness for the child in question. The four special circumstances envisaged are:

(i)   if the child has a medical condition likely to affect future learning ability;

(ii) if the child has been admitted in connection with a social condition which is likely to affect future learning ability (such as social deprivation, whether negligence, neglect or child abuse);

(iii) if a child is receiving treatment likely to affect his future learning ability;

(iv) if the child has been admitted to a children's or adolescent psychiatric ward.

9.4. Under Education (Special Educational Needs) Regulations 1983, LEAs must seek educational, medical and psychological advice relating to a child with potential special educational needs, together with advice *from any other source* which they consider desirable in making an assessment under Section 5 of the 1981 Act. Advice is interpreted as written advice on any features of the case which are relevant to or which affect the child's special educational needs and on the best way of meeting these needs. Some LEAs have drawn up their own structured forms for the collection of information on particular children. LEAs must provide all professionals with copies of any representations or views submitted by or on behalf of a child's parent. Parents have the legal right to see all advice used in drawing up a statement. The LEA has the final responsibility for collecting and collating such advice (which may include advice from the SSD) and in making decisions about any special educational provision which may be required. In making its decisions, an LEA must have considered:

(i)   educational, medical and psychological advice;

(ii) any evidence from the child's parents;

(iii) any information or advice provided by a DHA or SSD;

(iv) any other relevant advice.

9.5. Where a statement results, copies of all these documents must be appended to it, since the information forms part of the statement. The statement should, therefore, provide a comprehensive picture of the child and his or her needs which extends beyond the specific educational purpose of the assessment process. Where SSDs have parental responsibility for a child, they will have a dual role. Firstly they should play the part of a good parent. Secondly they should ensure that a social services contribution is made to the assessment. Although not all children in need – or indeed children with disabilities – will have special educational needs which cannot be met without a statement some will come within both groups and more effective participation in assessment under the 1981 Act should therefore be a priority for SSDs.

NOTIFICATION OF SSDs BY THE LEA

9.6. When the LEA notifies the parent of their decision to assess formally a child's special educational needs, a copy of the notification must be sent to an officer nominated for this purpose by the SSD. This is intended to offer the SSD an opportunity to consider whether they know of any problems affecting the child relevant to that authority and the range of services it might offer and to indicate to the LEA whether the social services has information relevant to the assessment of a child's special educational needs. Any advice provided by the SSD will be attached as an appendix to the statement. Parents have a right to see such advice. The LEA may also seek advice from the SSD of their own accord.

9.7. The notification of SSDs by LEAs may be an important opportunity for the SSD to meet with and inform parents of children in need with disabilities at a very early stage and to provide information about available services. This notification offers one of the few formal bridges between the two authorities and is an opportunity to link educational assessment to the assessment of a wider range of personal, social or health needs.

PROVISION OF INFORMATION

9.8. Under Section 10 of the Education Act 1981, DHAs must notify parents of children under five of any relevant voluntary organisation which would be likely to help them. Information provided by SSDs with regard to provision for children in need under the Children Act could usefully be made available to DHAs to give to parents when making such a referral. In any event DHAs and SSDs will frequently be working together in supporting particular children and families and a collaborative approach is likely to be the most helpful.

9.9. Under Section 10 of the 1981 Act, health authorities also have a duty to inform LEAs of any children under five who might have special educational needs. This procedure has resulted in earlier cooperation in meeting special needs. Although Section 10 of the Act does not refer to social services departments, they will need to work with health and education with reference to this section of the Act, as it will directly relate to the efficiency of registration procedure and the establishment of a joint register.

PARENTAL INVOLVEMENT

9.10. Parents have greatly enhanced rights to participation in assessment and subsequent special education provision under the 1981 Education Act procedures. They will see all copies of any professional advice made with regard to the assessment; they may contribute their own written comments on their child's special needs and their preferences and they have rights of appeal to a local appeals tribunal if they are unhappy with the outcome of assessment. However, some parents do not participate as fully as they might in assessment without support. In some instances, particularly where the family have a range of needs unrelated to the educational assessment, SSDs or voluntary organisations could support parents in assessment. An important outcome of such partnership could be a strengthened understanding of the needs of child and parents and an opportunity to learn from the wider advice on the child's medical and psychological as well as social and educational needs. When a child is subject to a care order, the local authority should also ensure that firstly, it involves anybody with parental responsibility for the child in any assessment procedure (supporting them in travelling to an assessment if necessary) and secondly, that it also acts as a good parent and contributes positively to assessment and encourages the child or young person to do likewise.

REVIEWS OF STATEMENTS OF SPECIAL EDUCATIONAL NEEDS

9.11. Every Statement of Special Educational Needs must be annually reviewed. Although SSDs are not necessarily involved, every effort should be made to ensure that a relevant member of social services (normally the child's social worker) attends the review of a child looked after. This will ensure that the department is informed of the child's progress and of any special difficulties which the school may be encountering. If there is anxiety about the arrangements made for the child, then reassessment may be requested.

UNDER FIVES

9.12. Section 6 of the Education Act 1981 places duties on LEAs with regard to children with special educational needs under the age of 2. Section 4(2) of the 1981 Act gives LEAs special responsibilities towards children with special educational needs from the age of 2 to the end of compulsory school age. The early identification of special educational needs is crucial for the young child with disabilities and/or delayed development as prompt suitable provision right from the start can considerably enhance the child's future progress. Circular 22/89 states that 'LEAs should give priority to children with special educational needs in admitting children to nursery provision' and emphasises the importance of liaison with school health and social services during the process. Precisely because many local authorities now operate Portage or other home based learning programmes or peripatetic teaching service, early referral to the LEA is essential for young children and parents. Additionally many LEAs provide advisory and support services to social services daycare provision (for example through the school psychological services). The Children Act contains important new provisions to help LEAs and SSDs work in a co-ordinated way. The new review duty – section 19 in Part III – requires the two departments to work together in looking at the pattern of day care services in their area, consulting DHAs and others and finally publishing a report. The legislation requires the review to be undertaken every three years, and Volume 2 of the Children Act 1989 Guidance and Regulations makes it clear that the process should involve follow up so that it is not to be treated as a one off exercise. The new legislation on the regulation of independent day care services and childminding – Part X of Schedule 9 to the Act – give SSDs power to ask the LEA for advice if it seems to them it would help them in the exercise of their functions under this Part. These provisions in the Act will make co-ordination and co-operation easier to achieve and thus help to ensure acceptable standards of services for all children.

ASSESSMENT OF CHILDREN IN SOCIAL SERVICES SETTINGS

9.13. DES has issued a circular and Regulations on the approval of Independent Schools to admit pupils with statements of special educational need (DES 2/91 and SI 1991 No 449). A child placed in a specific setting with an existing statement of special educational needs will already have considerable information on record about his needs. The identification of an actual or potential learning difficulty when the child is already placed in a care setting requires staff training and should be covered by clear procedures with regard to notification of the appropriate people and agencies.

9.14. If a child's special needs are identified when already using a day care or residential service provided by social services, the LEA may wish to carry out part of the assessment in the setting which is most familiar to the child. Parents may be very anxious and distressed at the potential identification of a disability or learning difficulty and will need counselling and support. Both care staff and parents should have accurate and clear information on the assessment process and should be aware of the possibility of a special need before any formal assessment arrangements are initiated. Social services staff (and those working in voluntary and independent settings) sometimes feel concerned but inadequate at participating in a primarily educational assessment. But parents and staff working with children observe and assess children. They learn from their behaviour, their preferences, their daily routines and they are likely to be able to predict behaviour in certain situations. They can provide invaluable information for assessment if encouraged to do so. As noted elsewhere change in the educational arrangements of a child may produce difficult behaviour and problems at school which may be short-term in the first instance, but predictive of longer term difficulties and failures if not dealt with promptly.

9.15. Since schools are also sources of social networks for children – and may provide consistent and positive role models for very disadvantaged children – every effort should be made not only to sustain a child's educational placement so that there is familiarity with his or her needs, but also to enable SSDs to work with the education services and to share knowledge and expertise in planning the best way forward. Participation by social services or other care staff can extend to a range of activities which an ordinary parent might expect to share. It should also include participation in home/school activities such as paired reading schemes or sharing in school-based social and other activities. Many schools now operate records of achievement for children and every effort should be made to ensure that children and young people with disabilities are enabled to contribute positively to recording their own achievements and progress and planning for the future. When a child is being formally assessed for a possible Statement of Special Educational Needs, staff working closely with a child should be encouraged to make their contribution to the assessment process and should have access to development checklists, local authority guidelines and any material locally developed to help parents carry out a similar exercise.

INTEGRATION

9.16. Both the Children Act 1989 and the Education Act 1981 place emphasis upon the importance of integration within mainstream provision for children with special needs wherever possible. SSDs, in considering placements for a child with a disability, should therefore take account of the educational arrangements which would accompany such a placement and make every effort to ensure that children can attend an ordinary local school or a local special school if this is regarded as the most positive option. The success or otherwise of an integrated placement will in part depend upon positive attitudes and expectations. But such attitudes are insufficient without a clear understanding of the needs of the child and the best way to meet them. The Fish Committee (1985) noted that:

'The concept of integration as a dynamic process is difficult to grasp. It is often confused with physical location and discussed in terms of specific situations rather than the whole life-styles of children. Integration is about planned interaction between a child and his or her environment and is not about changing the concept of special educational needs but about its context.'

9.17. SSDs and LEAs have new opportunities to use the Children Act 1989, the Education Act 1981 and the Disabled Persons Act 1986 in tandem to ensure well coordinated services for children with disabilities and special needs. In particular SSDs should be aware that an appropriate and early diagnosis of a child's difficulty in learning may be as important to that child's and family's future as a medical diagnosis or the provision of practical support to the family. Poor quality school work arising from family problems which are unknown to the teacher, difficulties in communication or unacceptable behaviour quickly isolate children and lead to a rapid erosion of self esteem and confidence. Equally a child's capacity to develop educationally will be directly affected by adverse home circumstances or unmet health needs. It is therefore crucial to link assessment processes under the Children Act 1989 and the Disabled Persons Act 1986 clearly to assessment under the Education Act 1981 (and under the NHS and Community Care Act 1990) – to ensure a collaborative – and thereby a more cost effective – response to individual children's special needs.

EDUCATION SUPERVISION ORDERS

9.18. The Children Act introduces a new system of education supervision orders which a court may make on the application of any LEA. The order replaces the previous provision under which children could be taken into care as a consequence of truancy, and offers one means of dealing with non-attendance at school when other arrangements have failed in securing regular attendance for the child in question. Provision for action against parents under the Education Act 1944 still applies. Education supervision orders appoint a designated person in the LEA to ensure – in conjunction with parents – that a child receives a proper education. The order is made under section 36(3) of the Act, if a court is satisfied that the child concerned is of compulsory school age and is not being properly educated.

9.19. The education supervision order was introduced because of a growing recognition that non-attendance at school was an insufficient reason for removing a child from the family home – not least because of the origins of school refusal were often school based or reflected differences of perception between school and family about how best to manage a particular child. The new order will be put into effect by an educational supervisor, whose duty it will be to advise, assist, befriend and give directions to the supervised child and parents in order to enable the child to be properly educated.

9.20. The wishes of parents and children must be sought before any directions are given. In the case of a child with disabilities not attending school, every effort should be made by the LEA and the SSD to discuss with parents why they are reluctant to use a particular school and what their wishes and concerns are. In some instances refusal may reflect concerns over assessment of special educational needs under the Education Act 1981 and anxieties about the use of a particular school, when another is preferred. Many parents have themselves had poor experiences at school and without support, will be unable to negotiate with a school about non-attendance, difficult behaviour or their own reluctance to agree to a particular provision. If non-attendance is linked to assessment, parents may need an independent adviser and counsellor to talk through the different options and their own contribution to the assessment process.

9.21. Non-attendance may also be due to purely practical reasons, such as difficulties with transport or when the parents feel that the school is unable to cope with their child's particular special needs – for example through the provision of suitable equipment or adaptations or sufficient supervision in the classroom. Whether these parental perceptions are wholly accurate is less important than the fact that school non-attendance has serious long-term consequences for child and family and every effort should be made to advise and support parents in resolving difficulties before a child has lost substantial periods of time from his education. If conciliation proves impossible and a supervisor is appointed, he should have knowledge of disability or special needs or access to specialist advice and be sensitive to the additional issues which may affect parental and child perceptions of provision offered. If the education supervisor is not able to achieve school attendance in partnership with child and parents, the Children Act gives the local authority further powers to intervene on behalf of the child. But the new process should provide a new opportunity for a more constructive relationship between families, schools and the local authority over school attendance – and a better understanding of the reasons why parents and children sometimes resist regular school attendance.

YOUNG PEOPLE OVER 16

9.22. Under section 5 of the Disabled Persons Act 1986, LEAs must obtain an opinion from the SSD as to whether a child is or is not a disabled person as part of the first annual review or assessment or reassessment after the child's 14th birthday. LEAs are required to notify SSDs 8 months before the date when a young person with disabilities is likely to leave full-time education, and to keep the date under review. SSDs are required to carry out a multi-disciplinary assessment within 5 months of the LEA notification unless the young person or parent does not want it. In addition, Regulation 9 of the 1983 Regulations prescribes that where the LEA maintain a statement in respect of a child whose educational needs have not been assessed since before the child reached the age of 12 years and 6 months, they should reassess those needs during the period of one year beginning with the day on which the child reaches the age of 13 years and 6 months. This provides the opportunity for the child, and all concerned with his future, to consider the arrangements to be made for the remainder of the child's time at school and for preparation for transition to adult life, and to determine the nature of the further education, vocational training, employment or other arrangements to be made.

CHAPTER 10 THE ROLE OF CHILD HEALTH SERVICES

10.1. The SSD's role with regard to children with disabilities and their families under the Children Act cannot be effectively implemented without close partnership with child health services. The role of the SSD cannot be fulfilled unless it is fully understood by the local health services, and unless there are shared arrangements for the transfer of information about children and joint planning for their futures. In addition to identification and assessment, children and young people with disabilities will have a range of other health care needs including health promotion advice which should be considered when planning for their futures. All DHAs have surveillance and prevention programmes agreed with the appropriate FHSAs, although the arrangements will vary according to local policy and practice. SSDs now have to consider health and development as part of their assessment of children in need and they should be aware of local policies and practice on child health surveillance. The Court Report (1976) described surveillance as including five main areas of activity, namely:

(a) the oversight of the health and physical growth of children;

(b) monitoring the developmental progress of all children;

(c) providing advice and support to parents or those caring for the child, and referral of the child to appropriate services;

(d) providing an effective immunisation programme against infectious diseases; and

(e) encouraging parents to participate in health education and training for parenthood programmes.

10.2. Although there is continuing debate about the effectiveness of some developmental screening tests undertaken as part of child health surveillance, there is consensus that prevention and surveillance should be closely integrated within a comprehensive child health service embracing primary and secondary health care services. Children with disabilities should be identified at an early stage through access to effective surveillance programmes. SSDs should be aware, therefore, of the contribution to be made by child health services to the early identification of children in need and should ensure that children looked after by them – or children who receive services from the SSDs – have access to good quality locally provided health care (see Chapter 2 of Volume 3: Family Placements for detailed guidance on health care arrangements for looked after children). Children with disabilities are children first and should have access to the same services for health surveillance and promotion as are available to children generally.

10.3. SSDs should liaise closely with their child health services counterparts not only to encourage parents to share in recording their child's development and health care needs, but also to ensure that where children in need are identified parents and child can contribute to decisions on the type of care and support provided to the family. For example, parents of a child with multiple disabilities may find attendance at a local clinic impossible without day care arrangements for brothers and sisters. In order to inform themselves of local policy with regard to early identification and surveillance and prevention, SSDs could usefully create links with local child development centres or teams and any other services which work directly with a wide range of families. Prevention – and surveillance – are multi-factorial and social services staff (including those working in day care provision and as foster parents and childminders) should also understand local arrangements for early support from child health services and the importance of ensuring that children with disabilities use these services.

10.4. The full benefits of early identification and the register of children with disabilities will only be achieved if there is a genuine partnership between DHAs and, in some areas, NHS Trusts and SSDs. DHAs already have duties under section 10 of the Education Act 1981 to inform LEAs of any child under five years of age who might have special educational needs. Anxieties expressed by many parents about the association between SSD intervention and the diagnosis of potential child abuse will necessitate open and honest discussion between parents, carers, SSDs and health service staff about the role of the individual agencies and their agreed procedures for transfer of information. Indeed transfer of information is unlikely to occur unless the DHA and parents have clear intelligible and relevant information on the Children Act and unless parents are confident of the purpose and subsequent use of the register.

10.5. Under the Education Act 1981, DHAs and SSDs are required to contribute medical and social services advice to the Statement of Special Educational Needs, under a section 5 assessment. Although the purpose of such an assessment is to identify the educational special needs of the child, the assessment process will be a useful additional source of information about the child who receives help both from the SSD and the DHA. In such cases, joint discussion should take place on the relevance of the information contained in the medical advice for the future planning of services.

10.6. Child health services have an important role to play in assessment of a child's needs in the context of a proposed day care, residential or foster placement. Disabilities which carry special health care needs, should not be regarded as automatic barriers to integration and use of local children's services. In many instances advice from child health services on, for example, the management of anti-convulsant medication can reassure a foster family, childminder or teacher so that a child need not be removed from local community provision, including schooling. The child health service has an important role in providing relevant and helpful information which can facilitate the integration of children with disabilities in the community. Steps should be taken to forge links between the general medical practitioner, the hospital paediatrician or other specialist medical service, so that medical information is collated and interpreted for the benefit of the child and family. The child health service is also in a position to ensure that referral is made to paramedical services, which in turn can support the child's integration into local services. The role of GPs, health visitors and community nursing services is crucial to the effective support of many vulnerable children at home. SSDs should endeavour to work closely with such services and acknowledge their important and non-stigmatising role in dealing with a wide range of needs relating to general parenting problems as well as to needs specific to a child's disability or chronic health problem. One way of facilitating such cooperation and effective coordination is for active SSD involvement in and representation on child development/district handicap teams and community mental handicap or learning disability teams.

CHILDREN WITH LIFE THREATENING CONDITIONS

10.7. Some children have major health care needs or life threatening conditions. In these cases child health services, in addition to providing medical services, will also provide advocacy and personal support for the children and their carers. The wishes and feelings of the child should be of paramount importance – with many children wishing to talk to supportive and well informed medical advisers about the management of their condition and the prospects for the future. Sensitive suport, including counselling, home nursing and the provision of appropriate respite care, may enable families who wish to continue to care for their children at home through the duration of their illness including the terminal stage. In some areas children's hospices, which may offer a combination of residential, respite and domiciliary care, provide a useful complementary service. The management of very sick children – or those with very complex disabilities – will require a holistic approach which involves the DHA, LEA, SSD and often the voluntary sector in planning with the child and his family for the future. A real partnership between all involved agencies and the parents and child wherever possible should ensure that a range of services used by children generally is available in addition to those services specific to children with chronic and life threatening conditions. It should also ensure that children with disabilities receive care and support in the home. Where it is not possible for a child to remain at home, they should be placed in residential settings where their specialist health care needs can be met (for example physiotherapy) and where access to specialist health care advice (for example a paediatric neurologist) is readily available. Staff in children's services (including residential staff and foster families) may need support in continuing to care for very vulnerable children. Paragraph 4.38 of **The Welfare of Children and Young People in Hospital (HMSO 1991)** contains further guidance.

PLANNING FOR THE FUTURE

10.8. In making arrangements for the ongoing care of young people with disabilities, every effort should be made to ensure that any health care needs are planned for in the transition to adult life. Cooperation in managing transition is essential and SSDs should consider carefully how they liaise with the schools health services, special schools and with child development or district handicap teams, where attachment of a social worker may provide a constructive link between DHAs, LEAs and SSDs in planning for the future (see Chapter 16).

CHILDREN LIVING IN NHS PROVISION

10.9. In some cases, for children with substantial medical, paramedical and nursing needs the health service will still have a continuing role in the provision of respite and longer term residential care. This is ultimately best decided through multi-disciplinary assessment properly involving parents and child. The use of NHS provision should be part of a planned programme of support for the individual child. Every effort should be made to support placements in local community provision with appropriate input from the NHS. It is clear government policy that children with a learning disability should no longer live in long-stay mental handicap hospitals. Instead, where NHS provision is required, the aim should be to provide care in small, homely, locally-based units. The Welfare of Children and Young People in Hospital guide (HMSO 1991) should be made available to staff in social services, education departments and child health services to ensure that any care provided is appropriate to the needs of children and the general provisions of the Children Act (see also paragraphs 13.7–13.13). Hospital based social workers are well placed to contribute to the continuing assessment of the health and social care needs of children in hospital and to give practical advice and support.

CHAPTER 11 ACCOMMODATION AS A SERVICE

11.1. The Children Act intends accommodation to be provided, wherever possible under voluntary arrangements, as a service to children in need and their families. The Act assumes a high degree of co-operation between parents and SSDs in negotiating and agreeing what form of accommodation can be offered and the use made of it. Where a child with disabilities is provided with accommodation by a SSD, the Act requires that, so far as is reasonably practicable, the accommodation should not be unsuitable to the needs of the child (section 23(8)). For example, the SSD may wish to provide for suitable adaptations to a foster parent's home. By including children with disabilities in the category of children in need, the Children Act requires SSDs looking after children in need to apply the same planning and review arrangements to them as are needed for other children in need.

11.2. Volume 3 in the Children Act series, **Family Placements** contains regulations and guidance relating to the planning and review of placements of children looked after by a SSD or accommodated by a voluntary organisation or in a registered children's home (all "responsible" authorities) including foster placements. The regulations and guidance provide a statutory framework for the planning and agreeing of arrangements for placement of a child and require pre-placement enquiries and preparation and subsequent supervision and monitoring of the placement. The regulations also define their application to short-term placements. Decisions made about placement must take account of the wishes and feelings of the child, the parents and any others with parental responsibility and any other relevant people. Such decisions must have regard to the child's religion, racial origin, culture and language. Responsible authorities should endeavour to place children with parents, relatives or friends, near their homes and with brothers and sisters.

11.3. As well as stating that accommodation for children with disabilities should not be unsuitable for their needs, the Act says that services should minimise the effects of a child's disability. Planning a placement for a child with a disability who will be living away from home should follow the same principles for placements which would apply to a child without a disability. All children need arrangements which offer them a sense of permanence and security; which whenever possible provide an experience of ordinary family life; ensure that appropriate education is available and encourage the child to develop a positive self-image and to enjoy the same opportunities for personal growth as would be available to other children without a disability. SSDs should not lose sight of the need to establish who exercises parental responsibility for the child on a day to day basis. Every effort should be made to ensure that children are not placed far from their family home and local community. If the use of such provision is essential, family links should be maintained and encouraged. The child and his relatives should be enabled (through financial support if necessary (see 11.5–11.6)) to maintain a good relationship. SSDs should seek to involve parents where they have become peripheral to the child's life. Children with disabilities may be among the most vulnerable children in terms of creating and maintaining family and community links. Their views may not be actively sought because of misconceptions about their level of ability to understand and communicate (see paragraph 6.6–6.8). As for all children, attention should be given to issues relating to racial origin, gender, cultural and linguistic background and religion – and to the child's preferences and personal aspirations and interests.

11.4. Misunderstandings about decisions are most likely to arise when children and young people have become isolated and little is known of their former life-style and family and social networks. Talking with children right from the start is an essential and integral part of any participation strategy and should be a key factor in planning services for particular children with disabilities.

PROMOTING CONTACT

11.5. When a child is looked after by the SSD they must endeavour to promote contact between the child and parents, relatives and friends and anyone else connected with him (paragraph 15 of Schedule 2 to the Act). The SSD also has a duty to promote contact between children in need and their families where the children are not accommodated by the SSD but are living apart from their family, if it is necessary in the opinion of the SSD to safeguard or promote the child's welfare (paragraph 10 of Schedule 2). If parents feel guilty or ambivalent about the residential placement – or if the cost of visiting is high – relationships may also suffer. One important consideration in any foster care or residential placement is reunification of child and family. This is more difficult to achieve if contact with parents and other significant figures in the child's life such as friends, brothers and sisters, relatives from the extended family or other people in the local community is lost.

11.6. Promoting contact should be seen as an integral part of a placement plan. SSDs should assist the family, relatives and child with travelling expenses where they consider that there would be undue financial hardship if assistance was not given and the circumstances warrant it (paragraph 16 of Schedule 2). Families may feel inadequate and uncertain about maintaining links with a child in a residential setting. Encouragement and a positive welcome to visits on a regular basis are therefore extremely important. Similarly residential care and foster family members should be reminded of the importance of their role in reunification by promoting the child's links with home through letters, phone calls, visits and open days. More detailed guidance on contact is contained in Volume 3: Family Placements.

THE INDEPENDENT VISITOR

11.7. Many children with disabilities who need a residential service are placed at some distance from their family home, because of problems in finding acceptable accommodation with the necessary specialist facilities. Paragraph 17 of Schedule 2, enables local authorities to appoint an independent visitor (see Chapter 7 of Volume 3 for further guidance). In general, such an appointment will not be made unless the child has not been visited by his parent or other people with parental responsibility for over a year. The appointment of an independent visitor should only be considered when all the possible means of promoting contact with the child's family or friends have been explored, and the assistance provided by the SSD has demonstrably failed to ensure regular and beneficial contact between child and family. If it is then judged to be in the child's best interests to have such a visitor, an appointment of a visitor may be made who will visit, advise and befriend the child. Expenses incurred during these visits may be recovered from the SSD.

11.8. Independent visitors offer an important opportunity to maintain contact between a child or young person with a disability and his local community. In a very limited number of cases there may be a relative who would be appropriate to fulfil the role of independent visitor and this arrangement might be the child's preferred option. SSDs will need to distinguish between the small minority of cases where the designation of a relative or friend as the child's visitor is appropriate and the more common situation where the child properly has ongoing contact with relatives and friends. In the latter situation the SSD should encourage such contacts and may pay expenses without the necessity of changing the status to that of independent visitor (paragraphs

15(1) and 16(2) of Schedule 2). Children may object to a particular appointment or they may be able to suggest who might perform such a role.

11.9. Every effort should be made to ensure that the independent visitor is not only acceptable to the child, but that he is familiar with the child's special needs and can communicate – if necessary through Makaton or in sign language. A visitor may need guidance and support in identifying what key factors to consider in the child's environment and how to establish a relationship with a child with complex needs. Children should have opportunities to see their independent visitor in private if they so wish and the visitor's views on the current lifestyle and feelings of the child should be considered carefully by the appointing SSD. In appointing suitably experienced independent visitors, SSDs might choose to liaise with their relevant voluntary sector to ensure that visitors (if unknown to the child) do have a clear understanding of the child's disability and its likely impact on the child in question.

PLANNING

11.10. Under the Children Act regulations assessing and planning for a placement will be reinforced and updated by regular reviews which take account of the child or young person's views, with those of parents and others. Parents who retain parental responsibility for the child during a placement, should also be actively encouraged to plan for the child's future. Many families find relationships with carers very difficult to cope with and may perceive a residential or foster placement as family failure. Involvement of parents during the planning stage and subsequent placement is essential to the success of the placement and to any longer term plan for the child's return to his family.

SHORT-TERM OR RESPITE CARE

11.11. Respite care should be provided in the context of a package of care for families. Many children with disabilities are cared for away from home or usual placement on a short-term basis as part of a planned programme of respite care. Respite or short-term care for families with a child with disabilities has developed historically as an emergency service – frequently providing short-term care within a long-stay hospital or other institution in order to meet a family crisis. In the past decade there has been growing concern to provide more appropriate flexible short-term care which offers:

- a local service, where the child can continue to attend school as if still living at home;
- Good quality child care in which parents have confidence and which ensures that the child is treated first as a child and then for any disability which may require special provision;
- Planned availability. Research into different models of respite care has clearly indicated the importance of parents (and older child) choosing patterns of use and being able to use a service flexibly;
- A service which meets the needs of all children. Concern has been expressed about the lack of respite care for children with complex needs. The service should be available to children living with long-term foster carers or adoptive parents;
- Care which is compatible with the child's family background and culture, racial origin, religious persuasion and language;
- Age-appropriate care – so that young children and adolescents are given relevant care and occupation; and
- An integrated programme of family support which sees planned respite care as part of a wider range of professional support services to meet family needs. Escalating use of respite care may indicate a need for other family support services.

11.12. Some children still receive such care in NHS provision. This may be appropriate where the child has substantial medical, paramedical and nursing needs. It is clear government policy that children with a learning disability should no longer live in long stay mental handicap hospitals. Instead if NHS provision is required the aim should be to provide care in small homely, locally-based units. However for most children care provided by SSDs or voluntary organisations will be appropriate with an input from child health services if required. There are examples of community facilities run by DHAs, SSDs and voluntary organisations, sometimes working in partnership, which achieve high standards of respite care.

11.13. A number of evaluations of respite care schemes have shown varied patterns of use by families, with some a few hours a week with occasional overnight stays and others, shared care arrangements in which the child spent regular periods away from home. It is important to acknowledge the stresses associated with the child using respite care for the first time and sensitive introductions are required.

APPLICATION OF REGULATIONS

11.14. The Children Act regulations relating to placements makes special provision for short-term placements within schemes which are variously known as respite care, phased care or family link schemes. Under such schemes, a SSD or voluntary agency makes arrangements for a child who normally lives with his family –and whose family continues to exercise full parental responsibility – to spend short or sometimes longer periods of time with either an approved foster parent or in a residential home. These regulations apply to all placements of more than 24 hours. The arrangements for respite care vary greatly and many schemes only make provision for day-time or occasional over-night stay. In these cases, if the provision of services to the family does not include accommodating the child for a period of more than 24 hours then the regulations relating to placements do not apply. However, good practice requires that all such provision is properly planned.

11.15. It is important to note that in respect of arrangements which do not involve a SSD initially that under the Children Act the private fostering provisions come into force after a child has been, or it is intended that he will be, living with a foster parent for more than 27 days. Up till then, the registration system regulating childminders applies. This requires the SSD to register a person who for reward cares for children aged under 8 on domestic premises, provided they are satisfied that the person is fit to care for such children. The Act requires SSDs to impose requirements on a registered person about the number of children he may care for, safety of the premises and equipment, records to be kept and notification of changes. In cases where parents make their own arrangements for respite care for their child by contracting with a childminder, they are responsible for ensuring that these are satisfactory although the SSD's responsibilities in respect of child minding will apply. It is important that SSDs' registration officers find out about child minders who intend to offer a respite care service so that the appropriate requirements are imposed on the person's registration. In such cases attention needs to be paid to the sleeping arrangements, the type of equipment available, training needs and information about other resources in the community.

11.16. Some children may spend longer periods of time away from home and, it is necessary from the start to clarify the purpose of the respite care, to plan for the child's use of a particular service and to acknowledge that respite care may not meet all the needs of the child and family. Respite care may be only one component of a package of services.

11.17. Regulation 13 of the Arrangement for Placement of Children (General) Regulations 1991 allows for a pre-planned respite care arrangement involving a series of placements at the same place to be treated as a single placement. For family placements, all placements should take place with the same carer.

For residential placements, all placements should take place at the same establishment. The length and timing of the individual placements within this arrangement need not be specified in advance, but all the placements should occur within a period which does not exceed one year, no single placement should exceed four weeks and the total time spent by a child in respite care should not exceed 90 days. The purpose of this provision is to allow the regulations to be applied once in relation to a series of placements if the conditions above are met.

11.18. Under the Arrangements for Placement Regulations, SSDs or voluntary organisations are required to have a plan for each child setting out the proposed respite care arrangements as required under these regulations. The Foster Placement (Children) Regulations 1991 apply in all other respects for family placements. Children may only be placed with an approved foster parent – but a foster parent may be approved if desired for a respite care scheme only and the chosen name of the scheme and the carers may be used within the agreement. There has been some concern that the new arrangements might over-formalise a service which has been designed to offer highly flexible and consumer-sensitive care reflecting the needs of a particular local community. However, the new regulations and guidance provide flexibility in their application to short-term respite care placements while seeking to ensure a child focused service. Regulations require medical examination of the child at stated intervals, but do not set out the form the examination should take nor whether it should be a child's GP or a consultant who should carry it out. This will be a matter to be decided in the individual case. The matter should be discussed with the parents, the child, the carers, the consultant responsible for the child and the GP if doubt exists about the most appropriate person to carry out the medical examination. It is envisaged that these examinations will be part of the usual health care arrangements for the child.

11.19. The formalisation of previously more informal arrangements is to safeguard the welfare of the child. Some parents perceive regulated foster care arrangements as relating to care proceedings and inadequate or uncaring parenting. Equally some of the families recruited for family-based respite care have never seen themselves as foster parents and may be alarmed at the prospect of a more regulated service. In practice all good family based respite care schemes have always operated upon a firm principle of written agency and parent agreements and planning around the individual needs of children. The recruitment and training procedures for respite carers should now include opportunities to explain the new basis of regulating respite care and the mutual advantages to children, parents and respite carers of having greater accountability for the service provided. Positive publicity should emphasise the advantages of working within a planned framework which supports both parents and carers.

CHAPTER **12** **FOSTER PLACEMENTS**

12.1. It is generally agreed that all children benefit from the opportunity to grow up in a family setting. Although finding a suitable foster family placement for a child with a disability may create certain challenges, the past decade has seen a major growth in successful foster placements for children with a range of special needs. While SSDs must take the lead, the contribution of the LEA and the DHA to assessment of needs and support in the placement will be crucial. A number of national voluntary agencies also provide specialist fostering programmes for children with disabilities.

12.2. Under the Children Act, there are three different types of fostering arrangements:

(a) Local authority foster parents;

(b) Foster parents with whom a child is placed by a voluntary agency; and

(c) Private foster parents.

Foster placements under the Children Act are governed by the Foster Placement (Children) Regulations 1991 which apply to foster placements by SSDs and voluntary organisations (see Volume 3: Family Placements for detailed guidance on foster placement). Without special exemption from the SSD, no person may foster more than three children unless the children concerned are all siblings from the same family.

RECRUITMENT OF FOSTER PARENTS

12.3. Recruitment campaigns may need to be targeted at particular groups in the community, especially where the SSD have a need for foster families from particular racial, cultural or religious groups and with practical experience of disability. Many foster families for children with disabilities may be identified among those who have had personal experience of disability through employment; local community work or relatives and friends. In addition to positive policies on recruitment, training and support programmes for foster families should include opportunities to meet children with disabilities and their parents, to visit local services (including schools) and to have practical information on particular disabilities and their management. Attitudes and expectations about the potential of children with disabilities will be directly affected by the arrangements for recruitment and training. The possibility of involving people with disabilities as foster parents or as contributors to training programmes should be actively considered. Many children with disabilities lack positive adult role models and will gain greatly from contact with adults with similar disabilities who are well integrated in their local communities and can give counselling and practical help.

12.4. Every effort should be made to avoid frequent changes in schools and to ensure that children are not disadvantaged by the use of placements which involve major changes in their educational experiences. Continuity in education should be seen as a high priority in making a placement. SSDs should ensure that potential foster parents understand the central role of parents and be willing to participate with parents in the social, academic and community activities of the school in question. Such involvement might mean:

(a) Sharing attendance at school activities such as open evenings, PTA meetings, assessment and reviews;

(b) Taking an interest in sharing school-based learning programmes such as paired reading schemes, home/school diary, speech or physiotherapy and independence training exercise;

(c) Taking up the facilities on offer for study – for example a fifteen year old approaching GCSE will require space and opportunity for private study and access to libraries, books etc;

(d) A willingness to maintain friendship links and to encourage the child to bring friends home, or to attend leisure activities or play-schemes where such friendships may be nurtured and developed. Some children with disabilities lead limited and often isolated social lives. Foster families should be asked if they are willing to help develop positive links with the local community and whether they have the time and commitment to support such networks.

TRAINING AND SUPPORT FOR FOSTER PARENTS

12.6. In addition to initial training after recruitment, foster parents will need specific training around the particular needs of individual children. Successful placement of children with disabilities will require understanding of the nature of the disability and its most effective management. For example, foster parents may need to know how to check and adjust hearing aids (or learn British Sign Language or use the Makaton Vocabulary or other communication systems where a child is deaf or has other communication problems). A child with cystic fibrosis will need help with postural drainage and any carer will need to understand the most effective way of managing respiratory tract infections and diet. Children with physical disabilities will not only need 'care' but active encouragement to develop self-care and independence skills. Children with learning disabilities similarly need support in acquiring new skills and in playing an active part in their local community.

12.7. Foster parents, like natural parents, will need supporting in acquiring the relevant skills. They should be encouraged to join local voluntary organisations for the relevant disabilities and to acquire any necessary skills through attending courses or using distance learning material such as those available through the Open University. Caring for a child with a significant disability can be tiring and foster families may feel isolated and concerned at how they balance other family commitments with a child's special needs. Many specialist foster schemes now offer respite care and access to day care and holiday play-schemes to foster families. Particularly if a child has complex or multiple disabilities (and special health care problems), every effort should be made to ensure that foster parents – like other parents – have information on the full range of services and are in contact with other parents and relevant professional and voluntary sources of help in the area. Many children with disabilities will regularly attend paediatric or other child health service departments. Whenever possible, placements should ensure a child's continued use of such provision and foster parents should be encouraged to be active partners with parents if appropriate, in such visits and any treatment arrangements.

THE FOSTER HOME

12.8. Foster families provide children with disabilities with an important opportunity to live in their local communities rather than be placed in more traditional forms of residential care. However, ordinary homes may be neither automatically accessible nor suitable for children with disabilities.

12.9. SSDs should make every effort to ensure that accommodation for a child with a disability is suitable for his or her needs. Section 23(8) of the Children Act requires that they "so far as is reasonably practicable, secure that the accommodation is not unsuitable to his particular needs." The provision of appropriate equipment or adaptations to bathrooms and bedrooms can make accommodation suitable and encourage independence. Where necessary, an occupational therapist can make an assessment of the child's future living environment and ensure that it is as barrier free as possible.

12.10. It is essential that children with disabilities (who may have incontinence or special personal care needs) should have privacy in bathroom and bedroom and that they should not be excluded from the main areas of the home such as living rooms and kitchen (and the social activities which take place in these areas) because of access difficulties. In many instances access problems can be resolved through the use of relatively simple and cheap modifications such as the use of moveable ramps and other aids. It is quite unacceptable for a child to be placed in a setting where he or she is more restricted than would have been the case in the natural home or in a residential setting. Similarly accommodation may be suitable in itself, but the child will be severely limited in his or her use of it if the carers lack confidence in the management of a child with, for example, a severe visual handicap or if the child concerned is hyperactive. SSDs should additionally ensure that the accommodation is safe for the child in question and that access (and egress) can be easily accomplished in the case of fire. If a child is hyperactive or for some other reason is liable to be at risk if playing outside the house, the safety of any garden gates and fences should also be assessed. It would be inappropriate for a child with a disability to have to be confined unnecessarily to particular rooms because of problems of safety relating to the physical environment of the placement.

DISCIPLINE AND SANCTIONS

12.11. Prospective foster families should be asked for their views about discipline and sanctions (including the arrangements which they use with their own families). The Foster Placement Regulations require that prospective foster parents agree not to use physical punishment on children placed with them as a condition of being approved as a foster parent. There should not be any restriction imposed on visits to or from parents or family members as a disciplinary measure. Foster parents may need advice and reassurance about how to manage difficult behaviour and what controls are acceptable in particular circumstances. Such advice and the opportunity to discuss different options in the management of difficult behaviour should be seen as an important and integral part of the training and support programmes provided.

PRIVATE FOSTERING

12.12. The provisions of Part IX of the Children Act in respect of privately fostered children relate in the main to children under the age of 16. *But in the case of a child who is disabled the age specified is under 18.* The SSD must be notified of all private fostering within their area.

12.13. SSDs have a duty to satisfy themselves that the welfare of children who are privately fostered is being satisfactorily safeguarded and promoted. They are also required to give advice if it seems to be needed. Particular attention should be given to situations where a child with a disability is being cared for on a private basis and where the carer may have little knowledge of or access to support services in the locality. Although private fostering is probably relatively little used for children with disabilities, there has been growing concern in some SSDs about children from overseas (usually families of students following professional or higher education courses in this country) when a developmental delay or special need is only identified when the child is actually in a placement. The inspection visits of all private fostering placements under the Children Act should ensure that such children have greater protection. The Children (Private Arrangements for Fostering) Regulations 1991 and associated guidance are contained in Volume 8 in the Children Act series.

CHAPTER 13 RESIDENTIAL CARE FOR CHILDREN WITH DISABILITIES

RESIDENTIAL CARE

13.1. Volume 4 in the Children Act series provides regulations guidance on children in residential homes and establishes important ground rules about the quality of the care and environment which should be provided. However, some children with disabilities will have special needs over and above those of their able-bodied peers. The availability of privacy and domestic-style living arrangements for children with disabilities may depend on access arrangements. Children with disabilities should have access to all the accommodation and the same rights to privacy as their able-bodied counterparts. For example, the management of incontinence or other personal care needs in an integrated setting will necessitate suitable bathroom accommodation which offers space, privacy, sufficient hot water and convenient location to other living areas. No child with a disability should be placed where he cannot use the recreation, living or garden areas because he can literally not gain access to them. Homes which accommodate children with a disability are required to provide the necessary equipment, facilities and adaptations. The aim should be to integrate the child in every aspect of life in the home, not merely the physical aspects.

13.2. Safety is an issue, particularly in older or adapted buildings which have accommodated relatively few children with disabilities. British Standards Institute publications (in particular BS 5588) give helpful guidance on access for disabled people. Careful attention should be given to the general fire precautions taken, including the nature of the furnishings and the arrangements made for fire drills and evacuations. For example, arrangements should enable children with physical or sensory impairments to be aware of and able to respond to fire alarms and evacuation of buildings. SSDs may find the **Child Accident Prevention Trust's Leaflet: Basic Principles of Child Accident Prevention** – A Guide to Action, useful.

CHILDREN ACCOMMODATED IN RESIDENTIAL CARE, NURSING AND MENTAL NURSING HOMES

13.3. Homes of this kind are registered and regulated under the Registered Homes Act 1984. The person carrying on such a home must notify the SSD if a child is accommodated either for three months consecutively or the intention of the person who decides to accommoate him is that he should stay that long. The SSD must also be notified when the child ceases to be accommodated (section 86).

13.4. The SSD has the same functions towards the child as are described below in respect of a child accommodated by a health or local education authority. The SSD is empowered to enter a residential care home, a mental nursing home or a nursing home in order to ascertain whether the children's welfare is being satisfactorily safeguarded and promoted (see Volume 4: Residential Care, paragraphs 195 et seq).

SECURE ACCOMMODATION

13.5. Under paragraph 7 of Schedule 2, every SSD must take reasonable steps to avoid the need for children to be placed within secure accommodation. However, in certain circumstances (section 25(1)) children may as a last resort be placed in secure accommodation (ie in accommodation which imposes restriction of liberty). A child may only be placed in such accommodation if:

(a) he has a history of absconding, is likely to abscond from any other type of accommodation and if he absconds is likely to suffer significant harm; *or*

(b) he is likely, if kept in any other type of accommodation, to injure himself or other people.

13.6. The provision and use of secure accommodation is governed by section 25 of the Children Act and by regulations made under that section the Children (Secure Accommodation) Regulations 1991. Section 25 and these regulations apply to children whose liberty is restricted in SSD, health authority and NHS Trust establishments other than under the provisions of the Mental Health Act 1983. A child cannot be so accommodated for longer than an aggregated period of 72 hours without a court order. For detailed guidance on the Children (Secure Accommodation) Regulations 1991 and on the provision and use of secure accommodation generally, see Volume 4: Residential Care.

CHILDREN ACCOMMODATED BY A HEALTH AUTHORITY, NHS TRUST OR LOCAL EDUCATION AUTHORITY

13.7. Although some children with disabilities or with serious health problems may spend substantial periods of time receiving care or treatment in an NHS facility, it is against government policy that such children should be placed for long-term residential care in a NHS hospital setting. The use of NHS facilities should reflect a child's need for assessment, treatment or other services which cannot be made in SSD provision or at home and should in no way constitute a permanent placement. Close working partnerships between SSDs and DHAs and NHS trusts should be an integral factor in local policies for implementation of the Children Act. Such partnerships will clearly identify the particular health care needs of individual children and the extent to which they should be met in a health setting. It should be emphasised that not all children with disabilities have health care needs. In many instances advice from child health services, with appropriate support, should enable children to continue to be cared for in SSD or voluntary provision.

13.8. In addition to treatment and ongoing assessment, there are some fairly rare circumstances in which it is necessary for children and young people to receive specialist medical care and treatment which can only be provided in a hospital setting (for example children with terminal or life-threatening conditions). Children's hospices are able to accommodate some of these children and such placements may be an important component in planned family support. If NHS provision is required the aim should be to provide care in small homely, locally-based units. However for most children care provided by SSDs or voluntary organisations will be appropriate with an input from child health services if required.

Notification Duty

13.9. If a child is provided with accommodation by a health authority, NHS Trust or LEA for more than three months on a consecutive basis or the intention is that this will happen, the health authority, NHS Trust or LEA *must* notify the responsible SSD. The responsible SSD is interpreted as being the SSD for the area in which the child lives or was ordinarily resident immediately before being accommodated or (if there is no such SSD) the SSD in whose area the accommodation for the child is being provided. The accommodating authority must also notify the responsible SSD (section 85(2)) when it is proposed to end the child's placement. The responsible SSD must take all reasonably practicable steps to enable them to decide whether the child's welfare is adequately safeguarded and promoted while he stays in the accommodation and to decide whether it is necessary to exercise any of their functions under the Act.

13.10. The intention of this new notification duty is to ensure that children are not 'forgotten' and that SSDs assess the quality of child care offered. Children with disabilities are more likely than other children to be placed in 'out of county' placements, frequently in remote and rural areas. The new arrangements should ensure more coherent planning for children and will necessitate close collaboration with child health services (including the specialist advice available through district handicap, child development and community mental handicap teams).

13.11. Where a child's stay in hospital is prolonged, the hospital social worker may have an important role to play. Chronic illness places enormous strain on a family's emotional and financial reserves. Counselling, practical and financial support (for example for hospital visits, baby-sitting etc) during and immediately after hospitalisation will do much to avoid longer-term problems. SSDs will need to work closely with health services including GPs and health visitors to support families when the child returns home. Guidance from the Department on The Welfare of Children and Young People in Hospital and guidelines from NAWCH (the National Association for the Welfare of Children in Hospital) are relevant.

13.12. Section 85 of the Act also requires DHAs, NHS Trusts and LEAs to inform the SSD of the area in which a child or young person proposes to live, if a child has reached sixteen and leaves accommodation which has been provided for at least three months (see Chapter 16).

13.13. Some children with disabilities and special needs attend independent or non-maintained residential special schools – some on a 52 weeks a year basis. The use of a residential school, after careful joint assessment by the LEA, the SSD and the relevant DHA may represent an important resource for the development of a particular child. Residential school placements should be made with a clear understanding of the nature and objective of the placement. Close links with the SSD in question will ensure that there is clear and coherent planning for the school holidays, the maintenance of family and community links and future arrangements for the child when leaving school. Placements in a residential school should never be made by SSDs without consultation with their LEA.

INDEPENDENT SCHOOLS

13.14. The Act gives new duties to SSDs with regard to the welfare of all children accommodated in independent schools. An independent school is defined as 'any school at which full-time education is provided for five or more pupils of compulsory school age, not being a school maintained by the local education authority, a grant maintained school, a non-maintained special school operated by a voluntary organisation nor a special school maintained by the education authority'. Schools with five pupils includes those which are primarily nursery schools but which happen to have any group of five children of school age. Hence private nursery schools which accommodate five or more children or young people of school age will come under the provisions of section 87(1) relating to the welfare of children accommodated in independent schools.

13.15. SSDs working in collaboration with health authorities or NHS Trusts as necessary must take all reasonably practicable steps to enable them to decide whether the child's health or welfare is adequately safeguarded and promoted in the school (section 87(3)). If they consider that the child's welfare is not being adequately safeguarded, the SSD may authorise people to enter the school in order to exercise their welfare duty and may under the Inspection of Premises, Children and Records (Independent Schools) Regulations 1991 inspect the school premises, records and the children. The right to inspect the children is of particular significance with regard to children with disabilities. They are the most likely to have communication difficulties and to be placed at some distance from their family home. Vigilance by SSDs will offer a significant new protection. HMI duties are unaffected by these new powers for SSDs.

CHAPTER **14** **COMPLAINTS PROCEDURES**

14.1. The Act requires SSDs, voluntary organisations and registered children's homes to establish procedures for considering representations (including complaints) about children's services. The procedure should cover all representations or complaints about a SSD's actions in exercising their functions under Part III of the Act (Local Authority Support for Children and their Families). Voluntary organisations and registered children's homes will also be required to set up representations procedures to consider representations or complaints made by or on behalf of children accommodated by them but not looked after by a SSD. The arrangements for such procedures are covered by the Representations Procedure (Children) Regulations 1991 (see Chapter 10 of Volume 3: Family Placements for detailed guidance). Representations and complaints which do not come under the Children Act procedure may be considered under the Local Authority Social Services Act 1970 procedure (section 7B as inserted by section 50 of the National Health Service and Community Care Act 1990 (see Caring for People: Community Care in the next decade and beyond Chapter 6 (HMSO 1990)) or may be more appropriately considered under another agency's procedure.

14.2. The principles behind the representation and complaints procedure are that children and other complainants should have access to a procedure which offers an opportunity to make statements about or to challenge decisions made by service providers and to ensure that the complaints procedure in question is fully understood and accepted by not only service users and their representatives but also by the SSD's or service providing agency's staff and the local authority's own elected members. Implementation plans should reflect the views of local consumer groups and service users and both should be involved wherever possible in setting procedures up so that they are confident that the system arrived at is fair, equitable and usable in the context of local needs.

14.3. Complaints and representations may be made about the way in which the SSD is acting in relation to a child in need, by the child, the child's parent or anyone having parental responsibility for him or her, any SSD foster parent or any other person who could be regarded as having sufficient interest in the child's welfare to warrant representations being considered by them.

14.4. The procedure developed by the SSD must have an *independent* element, which means that at the first stage of the procedure a person who is not a member or an officer of the local authority must take part in the discussion and consideration of such representations or complaints and in determining what action should be taken (section 26(4)). If the complainant is dissatisfied with the action the SSD propose to take after the first stage, the complaint may be referred to a panel with an independent element for further consideration. Local voluntary organisations and consumer groups may be able to provide nominations for panel members and can be a source of independent advice and advocacy for the child or family concerned. Every effort should be made to work with local disability groups to ensure that the procedures are accessible, useable and effective when dealing with issues relating to disabilities.

14.5. Authorities will be expected to give due consideration to the findings of those who carry out the complaints and representation procedure. They are not, however, bound to implement the findings. They will be required to notify in writing the person who made the complaint or representation, the child (if he has sufficient understanding) and anyone else likely to be affected by the SSD's decision, the reasons for it and what action (if any) they propose to take.

14.6. In the case of children with disabilities, complaints and representations are likely to focus around assessment and the delivery of (or failure to deliver) certain services. Because of the multiprofessional support needed by the majority of children with disabilities, the consideration of a complaint made by or on behalf of a child with disabilities should:

(a) consider whether there is a need to consult a range of relevant expert opinion, for example from the health authority or education department;

(b) ensure that children with disabilities are given appropriate support in making complaints or representations and in participating in decision-making about their own futures; and

(c) consider whether the complaint is really about another agency's services and should be directed to a different procedure.

14.7. There will be occasions when children or young people (and indeed many parents) will need help, advice or support from another individual or from an outside agency in framing or pursuing a complaint. Support should be offered or advice given on where support may be obtained, where a complainant is vulnerable or unsupported or where language, cultural diversity or a complex communication disorder or disability may impede communication. Many children and young people with sensory or learning disabilities will have more complex communication needs than can be met by the provision of an interpreter. If a written complaint is made or a verbal complaint recorded, they may not be easily able to verify the nature of the recording. Equally they are most unlikely to have easy access to information on complaints procedures which will be readily available to other potential users in the community. SSDs are required to give information on complaints procedures to children and young people with disabilities, with relevant and useable information about how a complaint may be initiated (particularly in a residential setting where access to a private telephone may be problematic). Schools may be a useful source of information for both children and parents. As noted above, complaints procedures should not be seen as the only way of resolving differences of opinion about services and management. Every effort should be made to use assessment and review in a positive and constructive way in order to negotiate a clearly understood package of services, with accurate information for all concerned about what is being provided.

14.8. In some instances complaints may relate to inappropriate services for children with disabilities, for example where there are poor access facilities, unsuitable furnishings or equipment or where children are unnecessarily excluded from the full range of activities appropriate to their ages, interests and general ability. In these instances expert advice on the particular disability should be identified eg from within the SSD, from a DHA or from a voluntary organisation and the SSD's existing arrangements for placement reassessed to avoid similar difficulties in the future.

14.9. It is essential that complaints procedures are explicit about how such vulnerable people may learn about complaints procedures and how they may use them, particularly if they are receiving services within their own homes. Section 26(8) of the Children Act requires SSDs to publicise their complaints procedures. This might be done in a variety of ways, ensuring that information is available in any relevant minority languages and that the local disability and users groups are part of the publicity process. SSDs might consider holding special meetings for their local voluntary sector to publicise the procedures and to ensure that the SSD and the consumer groups work in tandem in making the procedures work. Written information should also be freely available in SSDs, GP surgeries, hospital out-patients departments, health clinics, schools, libraries, nurseries, citizen advice bureaux and any other appropriate local setting used by the public. Because many people with disabilities have limited access to public buildings where such information is most likely to be prominently displayed, consideration should be given to how information on complaints procedures may be made widely available to parents of and children with disabilities.

CHAPTER 15 <u>CHILD PROTECTION AND</u> <u>COURT ORDERS</u>

15.1. The Children Act's emphasis on partnership and prevention is designed to enable family resources to be strengthened and for children to be brought up and protected within their own home if at all possible. The Act also provides for situations where parental care may have broken down and where the child is seen as suffering or likely to suffer from serious risk of ill-treatment (including both physical or sexual abuse). The essential element in the SSD's decision to apply to the court for an order will be lack of co-operation by parents in safeguarding and promoting the child's welfare. The balance between the rights of the child and the role of parents is at its most delicate in the field of child protection. Child protection is always complex and potentially contentious. In the case of children with disabilities, who may have communication or behaviour disorders, assessment of degrees of risk will be even more complex. But the Children Act offers new procedures which attempt to strike a reasonable balance between the need to protect children and the rights and responsibilities of any others involved. The legal effect of the new orders is clear and before making any order, including an emergency protection order or child assessment order, the courts must be satisfied that doing so would be better for the child than making no order at all.

15.2. The Children Act places a major emphasis on social work practitioners collaborating closely with other statutory and voluntary agencies which may have relevant knowledge of a child and family. Detailed guidance on child protection and court orders is in Volume 1: Court Orders. Guidance on inter-agency working will be contained in the revised **Working Together** – published in October 1991. The management, supervision, training and support of staff in education and health settings with children with disabilities will be critical for effective implementation of child protection policies and the early identification of children who may be at risk. Awareness of potential abuse in the disability field is comparatively recent, with a number of agencies developing new material and policies in this area.

15.3. The Children Act spells out the duties of SSDs to make investigations in a range of circumstances (section 47) to enable them to determine whether any action should be taken to safeguard a particular child. The options open to a SSD will vary according to the degree of risk to the child and the assessment of the extent to which those with parental responsibility are able and willing to cooperate in any plans for ongoing assessment and support. Relevant information must be provided by housing, education and health services unless regarded as unreasonable in the circumstances (section 47(10)). The Act states clearly that representatives of the SSD should try to see the child in the investigative process, unless they are satisfied that they have sufficient recent information (section 47(4)).

15.4. In considering the need to request a court order for a child with a disability, all agencies (whether within the local authority or not) must have clear views on what would be appropriate standards of health and development for the child in question. The use of court orders in place of earlier support and guidance for families would be against the principles of the Act. Careful baseline documentation will be essential and will require expertise and the involvement of appropriate professionals. Children who require considerable amounts of personal care, who have few communication skills or have severe learning disabilities will require very careful assessment. This group of children are particularly vulnerable to abuse and are the least likely to be able to articulate their fears or anxiety about inappropriate treatment. All statutory and voluntary agencies should ensure that their staff are aware of the inter-agency child protection procedure agreed by the Area Child Protection Committee (ACPC) in their area. Agencies should ensure also that their staff have information and training which will enable them to work responsibly if there is suspicion of a child being at risk.

CHILD ASSESSMENT ORDER

15.5. The child assessment order (section 43) is not an emergency order and notice is given between parties. It can be made on the application of a SSD or by an authorised person (for example the NSPCC), when the court is satisfied that:

(a) The applicant has reasonable cause to suspect that the child is suffering, or is likely to suffer, significant harm.

(b) An assessment of the child's health, development or of the way in which he has been treated is required to determine whether he is or is likely to suffer such harm.

(c) It is unlikely that an assessment will be made or be satisfactory in the absence of an order.

15.6. The court can allow up to 7 days for the assessment. The order must specify the date by which the assessment is to begin. The applicant should make the necessary arrangements in advance of the application, so that it would usually be possible to complete within such a period the medical or psychiatric examination or other assessment directed by the court. This should be sufficient to establish whether the child is suffering, or likely to suffer, significant harm and, if so, what further action is required. Because of the limited timescale for the duration of the order, the assessment arrangements must be well coordinated and the SSD should give careful advance consideration to the expert witnesses which it may want to call upon. In the case of a child with a disability, these may come from a very wide range of professionals; an educational psychologist or child psychiatrist may need to be involved. Parents may wish to bring their own expert witnesses but the court may rule on this. However, even at the late stage of going to court for an order the SSD should seek the parents' co-operation and agree on an expert to carry out the assessment and so avoid extra stress for the child. This needs to be considered in the context of:

(a) a new rule of court which requires any party to obtain the leave of the court before adducing evidence based on expert assessments.

(b) the duty on the SSD to ensure that the assessment is adequate for the purpose so as to fulfil its child protection responsibilities.

The court can direct the nature and type of assessment to be carried out and, in exceptional circumstances, may require that the child stay away overnight. This should, however, only happen very rarely.

15.7. Child assessment orders will, therefore, require the obtaining of information from a variety of sources about a particular child. Definitions of 'health' and 'development' may be particularly difficult in some children with multiple disabilities and complex behaviour patterns.

EMERGENCY PROTECTION ORDER

15.8. The emergency protection order is an emergency measure to provide immediate short-term protection. An emergency protection order gives powers to the applicant to remove a child to accommodation and to keep him there or to prevent his removal from the existing accommodation (for example a hospital ward). The order provides the applicant with parental responsibility for the child, but only in so far as the applicant needs it to safeguard or promote the child's welfare. Although the legislation provides for anyone to apply for such an order, the applicant will normally be the SSD or the NSPCC and in most cases the order will be transferred to the SSD after it has been made.

The order may only last for up to eight days unless extended for up to seven days by application to the court. The order may only be extended once. The original order can be made without notice and although there is no immediate opportunity to challenge it, there is the right to challenge the making of the order after 72 hours. This only applies if relevant parties were not given notice of the hearing and were not present.

15.9. Under section 46 of the Act, the police are given new powers to take a child into protection for up to 72 hours if the constable in question believes that a child might otherwise suffer significant harm. During this time the case must be investigated by a designated police officer ('the designated officer'). The constable in question must inform both the SSD and the child of what is happening and take reasonable steps to discover the wishes and feelings of the child. SSDs and the relevant police authority must have clear arrangements for dealing with any emergency protection order which concerns a child with a disability. Such arrangements should provide for expert advice to be available.

15.10 It is acknowledged that it is possible that misunderstandings about the most effective management of some children with disabilities (in particular those with challenging behaviour) may occur without clear understanding of the nature of the child's needs. However, children with disabilities are particularly vulnerable. They have the same rights as other children to be protected. At all stages it should be recognised that child protection procedures, however well they are managed, are traumatic for the child, his family and others caring for the child. Children with a disability should have clear explanations of what is happening and their views should be actively sought. Assumptions should not be made about the inability of children with, for example, severe learning disabilities or communication disorders to understand the procedures. With support and the advice of a known and trusted individual, the majority of children with disabilities can communicate their feelings and perceptions and articulate their needs. Children with disabilities, like other children, also have legal rights with regard to consent to treatment and the withholding of consent to medical examinations if they are judged to be of sufficient understanding to do so.

CONSENT TO TREATMENT OR EXAMINATION

15.11 Under section 43(8) of the Act, a child has the right to refuse to submit a medical or psychiatric examination or other assessment if he or she is regarded as having sufficient understanding to make an informed decision. The decision in the Gillick case (1986) established that children have a legal capacity to consent or not to medical examination or treatment if they have sufficient understanding of all that the examination or treatment entails. Such consent is not limited by a particular chronological age nor is it affected by disability or any other special needs. Where a child has a disability, however, special efforts should be made to explain the purpose and likely outcomes of any examination or assessment. Children may be particularly reluctant to agree to an examination if it involves unknown people in a strange place, or if they are frightened of the procedures involved. They should have the opportunity to discuss the proposed arrangements with a known and trusted person, if at all possible, who can reassure them and emphasise the need for an examination or treatment. If the child already has a Guardian ad Litem or a social worker, he will be involved in the discussion. Where children have communication difficulties these must be addressed. A child's refusal to consent to examination or treatment may be due to an earlier absence of real discussion with the child concerned about his feelings and anxiety about what has happened.

GUARDIAN AD LITEM

15.12 Since May 1984, courts have been able to appoint Guardians ad Litem in care proceedings, if the court is satisfied that there is a conflict of interests between child and parents. The principal function of the Guardian ad Litem is to safeguard and promote the interests of the child. The Guardian ad Litem has to conduct an investigation of the case independently to the SSD. The Guardian ad Litem will advise the court and make a recommendation as to whether a court order should be made or not. The Children Act builds upon the success of the Guardian ad Litem service, widens the range of court applications in which Guardians should be appointed and also strengthens a court's duty to provide a Guardian within that range. Under the rules of court one aspect of the Guardian ad Litem's function is reporting back to the court on whether the child is of sufficient understanding to refuse to submit to an examination or assessment. The Guardian ad Litem is also able to seek and present expert professional opinion.

15.13 Many Guardians ad Litem will have had limited experience of assessing the needs of children with disabilities. Those responsible for the management of the Guardian ad Litem panels will wish to consider how best to recruit Guardians ad Litem who have experience of working with children with special needs and who have special skills. Alternatively, the panel will need to provide assistance from people with skills, such as signing, which will be essential for communicating with children with communication difficulties.

CHAPTER **16** <u>**TRANSITION TO ADULTHOOD**</u>

16.1. Section 24(1) of the Children Act gives SSDs new duties to advise, assist and befriend each child whom they or certain other agencies look after with a view to promoting his welfare when he ceases to be looked after by them. SSDs are also reminded that they should take steps to prepare a child for the time when he is no longer looked after by them (see Volume 3 in this series – Chapter 9).

16.2. General improvements in services for young children with disabilities have led to increasing optimism about the feasibility of ordinary adult life experiences and independent living and employment. However, as the Warnock Report noted in 1978: 'We are aware that greater independence particularly for those with severe disabilities will not be achieved simply by administrative measures or the injection of more resources . . . in the end changes in the nature of education, training and supporting services will depend upon changes in *attitude*'.

16.3. The White Paper 'Education and Training for 21st Century' announced that both the duty to provide adequate facilities for further education and the duty to provide sufficient full-time education for all 16 to 18 year olds will transfer to the new Further Education Councils. LEAs will retain their duty to secure the provision of sufficient schools in the area for pupils of compulsory school age. When the sector is established, places for 16 to 18 year olds will be made available by LEAs (in school sixth forms) by the Councils (in former further education and sixth form colleges) and in grant-maintained schools and city technology colleges, but the duty to secure suitable full-time provision for 16 to 18 year olds will rest with the Councils. In fulfilling that duty the Councils will be required to have regard to the availability of places in schools. The Councils will also be required to have regard to the needs of those with learning disabilities.

The Need for Ongoing Support

16.4. All parents face problems in supporting and preparing their children for an independent adult life. Few young people (with or without special needs) are expected to become fully independent on their eighteenth birthday. The transition to financial independence and independent living is not usually a single event, nor does it happen quickly. The majority of young people achieve such independence in stages and many remain both economically and emotionally dependent upon their families in a variety of ways. Young people with disabilities are particularly vulnerable at the transition to adult life. If they have left SSD accommodation, they may all be the more vulnerable if there has been family breakdown or unhappy early life experiences. Some young people with disabilities may be vulnerable and ill equipped to cope with independence without ongoing support because their development may have been delayed in a variety of ways and they are less likely to have had access to the wide range of social experiences enjoyed by their non-disabled peers. They may have been over-protected and not provided with the same opportunities to develop independence as non-disabled young people have at a comparable age. In many instances they will need some degree of ongoing care and may be more dependent on other family members than they might choose. Additionally and importantly adolescence may bring full realisation of the longer term impact of disability on future job options and personal autonomy. In some instances disability may actually produce physical deterioration at this time. In other cases young people may become disabled through trauma or other injury and have to face adult life with the consequences of such injury.

16.5. Families also change at the time of transition. Parents themselves may be less physically able to cope or may have multiple family responsibilities with the additional care of elderly relatives. Brothers and sisters may leave home and families' capacity to care may be reduced. Importantly, the young people themselves may wish to leave home. Similarly it should be acknowledged that planning for adult life should take account of the real possibilities of assisted independence for many young people with disabilities and the importance of planning services which develop life skills and create real options for families. There are encouraging developments in independent living schemes, vocational training programmes and in community support for even severely disabled young people. Although investment in transition may appear expensive, the longer term benefits of greater competence and independence will be positive for everyone concerned.

16.6. To assist a young person with a disability to make a successful transition from childhood to adulthood requires that SSDs work closely with the youth service, schools and colleges to make certain that the arrangements are understood and also to identify any new needs. The local careers service should be involved in publicising information and also in identifying the full range of local services to which families might require access. It should also be stressed that in some instances the young people and their parents will need independent advice, counselling and advocacy in determining their needs and the most effective way of meeting them. For example, where a youngster has been in a residential school the holiday periods should be used to prepare the family for an eventual return home at the end of full-time education, or to test out alternatives explored as part of the review and planning process. Sometimes parents' and children's needs may appear to diverge when the young person grows older. Issues like the possibility of a move away from the family home, home adaptations or respite care should be explored in the light of the wishes and feelings of the young person and the family and should be given sensitive consideration. Where the young person comes from a minority ethnic group, efforts should be made to use every opportunity to identify the young person's and family's personal and cultural preferences. No assumptions should be made about what the parents or the young person want.

The Disabled Persons Act 1986 – Working with the LEA

16.7. Under the Education Act 1981, there is a statutory requirement that the LEA should reassess all pupils with Statements of Special Educational Needs at the age of thirteen years and six months, providing that they have not been formally assessed under section 5 of the Act after the age of 12 years 6 months. The purpose of this assessment is not only to determine the pupil's needs during his final years at school but also to begin the plan for post-school provision. It is therefore an important opportunity for the beginning of realistic forward planning for adult life, which should involve the child, the parents, the school, the DHA and the SSD in looking at a range of future options. Section 5 of the Disabled Persons Act 1986 requires LEAs to notify their relevant SSDs at the time of the first annual review of a statement following the child's 14th birthday, or at the time of a reassessment after that birthday, whichever is earlier. This notification is required so that the SSD may consider whether the child will require any future services from the SSD after they have left school. LEAs have a further duty to notify the SSD between twelve months and eight months before the actual date of ceasing full-time education. Section 5 then requires the SSD to carry out an assessment of the young person's needs, normally 3 months before he leaves school. This assessment should cover the whole range of need for social and welfare services, and the SSD are also expected, as far as possible, to give appropriate advice about matters such as employment and further education, and other services which may be available. This assessment and the consequent provision of services is of crucial importance in setting the scene for the young person's transition to adult life.

16.8. The past decade has seen major developments in education and training opportunities for young people with disabilities. SSDs could work constructively with education in considering what further opportunities for education and vocational training might be offered and should ensure that careers advice is given at an early stage. If mobility or access difficulties are going to be the real barrier to education or employment opportunities, every effort should be made to involve the occupational therapy and rehabilitation service at an early stage and to consider a range of options for encouraging access or personal mobility. In some instances a student may be able to attend an integrated course in further or higher education if he has some additional personal help. Although LEAs do fund ancillary and support workers in schools, this arrangement does not apply in further and higher education institutions. An appropriate use of monies made available through after-care might be to buy personal support to enable an individual student to attend the course most suited to his needs. Student financial support for study on full-time higher education courses – mandatory awards – provides allowances for students with disabilities who incur additional expenditure in respect of attending their course, including specific help to those in need of a non-medical personal helper, or requiring major items of equipment. LEAs are also able to offer discretionary awards to students with disabilities on other courses. The awards officers in the education department can offer further guidance. SSDs can also seek advice from organisations such as SKILL: the National Bureau for Students with Disabilities. Successful integration in educational or occupational training schemes will be ineffective unless the young person's home life is adequately resourced with appropriate aids and adaptations and the parents are given sufficient support to continue caring.

Collaborative Working

16.9. Planning for post-school provision will require careful assessment and ongoing planning. Parents and young people may have different preferences and views about where and when services should be provided. Realistic assessment should take account of the needs of both and should ensure that assessment takes account of the wider personal and social, health, occupational and vocational and educational abilities and needs of the young person in question. Education providers and their health authority counterparts will need to consider carefully how best to work together and with the young person and parents in planning for young people with disabilities. Patterns of collaborative working will vary across the country, but existing collaborative mechanisms in district handicap or child development teams, community mental handicap or learning disabilities teams and joint consultative committees may need reviewing or strengthening in order to ensure that young people have access to inter-agency expertise and provision.

16.10. Although different agencies' statutory responsibilities for children vary by age, authorities may wish to plan around existing team structures to provide support to young people beyond the statutory age of responsibility and to provide support during the transitional period to adulthood. Unless the resources and experience of children's services can be used during the transition to adult life, it is unlikely that young people's special needs will be met. Additionally existing resources and professional expertise will not be used in the most consumer-sensitive and cost-effective way and the skills developed during the school years may be lost in adult life.

16.11. The support of the primary health care team is of crucial importance to successful community care. SSDs should therefore ensure that they have precise arrangements for working with DHAs and FHSAs in order to ensure that joint planning is followed by joint service arrangements for young people with disabilities. Joint assessment and review cannot underpin more effective planning and care management if they do not involve all relevant agencies and professionals. GPs are crucial contributors to the assessment process. Their contribution to community care through knowledge of the whole family and the local community and their ability to monitor the individual young person's health and well being – as well as the delivery of general medical services – are essential in terms of support to young people living in their local community. For all young people the maintenance of good health is important. For children with disabilities the prevention of secondary handicaps or deterioration of an existing disability will require regular review.

16.12. The Children Act (section 27) provides for co-operation between housing authorities, SSDs, LEAs, DHAs and NHS Trusts. SSDs will need to liaise with housing authorities over the housing needs of young people with disabilities.

16.13. With regard to young people with disabilities, SSDs should consider their existing duties under the Chronically Sick and Disabled Persons Act 1970 and the Disabled Persons Act 1986. In some instances the ability of a young person with a disability to return home from a residential school or home – or to move into more independent living on his own – will depend not so much on the availability of accommodation but on the aids and adaptations that are provided to make existing accommodation suitable. Many young people with disabilities are severely limited by access problems in their own homes as they get larger and heavier. If the disability is degenerative or is acquired in the adolescent years, there may be major difficulties for all family members for example, because of use of living areas limited by access, and a consequent reduction in quality of life for the whole family. When the child has lived away from home for some years, reunification will be particularly difficult to achieve if the home is unsuitable and heavy burdens of care are suddenly imposed on the family.

16.14. The past decade has seen very encouraging development in independent living by a wide range of young people with special needs and disabilities. Many young people with learning disabilities, for example, are able to live together in supported independence in an ordinary house in their local community providing that they receive sufficient support. The support may be from an accessible and supportive adult, who can provide continuity and regularity of advice and guidance and ensure that the young people receive the financial support they need, that they acquire housekeeping and independent living skills and that they are encouraged to make the best use of the full range of neighbourhood facilities. Integration in the community depends on factors other than location and will require careful assessment, care management and regular review to be successful. Parents may feel very anxious about the ability of their son or daughter to live independently and they also will need support and guidance. Every effort should be made to ensure that parents and professional carers can work in partnership in supporting young people in becoming more independent.

16.15. Where a young person has very complex disabilities or where the family feel that they are unable to offer continued care, every effort should be made to find an acceptable local alternative. Residential care should not be regarded as a failure but as a positive option where parents, families and friends have a continuing role. With the cessation of admissions to long-stay hospitals for residential care, SSDs should consider as a matter of urgency how they can work in partnership with their health and education counterparts to develop new patterns of residential services which provide good quality care in the local community. Such care may be provided through SSDs, DHAs, voluntary or independent agencies or by combinations and consortia according to local provision. Wherever the young person is placed, SSDs, DHAs and LEAs will have a continuing role and every effort should be made to ensure that any placement encourages development and offers opportunities for continuing education.

16.16. Some young people will need additional educational opportunities, sometimes at residential colleges or schools outside their own local authority. The new arrangements for aftercare should enable education and SSDs to plan more coherently together to arrange and to provide funding for such arrangements. Specialist educational and vocational training will require clear planning agreements between the LEA and SSD.

The Wishes and Perceptions of Young People

16.17. Young people with disabilities and their families will need clear information on the full range of services in an 'easy to read' guide in order to begin to negotiate the most effective package of care. Access to local support groups and voluntary organisations will be particularly important. Many national voluntary organisations provide an 'outreach' service and can put individuals in touch with local self-help or self-advocacy groups for personal support and guidance. Self-advocacy and counselling should not, however, be regarded only as external services. A growing number of further education colleges, day centres and other provision for young people now have students' committees or associations. Many schools are moving towards student or pupil councils and the encouragement of informed decision-making and peer support from an early age. Every effort should be made not only to refer individuals to appropriate sources of help (whether within the voluntary or the statutory sector) but to ensure that there are opportunities for working together within the authority's own services.

16.18. Where a young person with a disability has been placed out of their local community, appropriate community support will be required. In some instances young people may not have any ongoing family relationships, and may, on leaving school find themselves living in localities where they have few personal contacts. SSDs should recognise the importance of relationship building and the need to assist such young people to develop friends and contacts in local communities. Every effort, therefore, should be made to begin planning at an early stage to maintain family and community links. Social work support and counselling may be able to recreate lost family and friendship networks, provided that such support is sensitive to changed life-styles and to real anxieties in some instances about the consequences of any reinvolvement.

16.19. In some instances, the young person's difficulties may result from diminished opportunities to discuss his or her disability and the various life options which might be available. Many young people express anxieties about their personal and sexual development and say they feel lonely and isolated. Realistic and sensitive counselling about future relationships and parenthood, possible implications of a particular disability and the help which may be available should all be addressed when appropriate. The support of a key worker who can provide continuity during the time of transition will be important. SSDs may wish to liaise with their local voluntary organisations in developing support networks and ensuring that parents and young people are aware of any local sources of independent advice or support in their area.

AIDE MEMOIRE: A RANGE OF SERVICES WHICH MAY BE PROVIDED BY SOCIAL SERVICES DEPARTMENT, LOCAL EDUCATION AUTHORITIES, DISTRICT HEALTH AUTHORITIES, HOUSING AUTHORITIES ETC AND THE VOLUNTARY AND INDEPENDENT SECTORS

SOCIAL SERVICES DEPARTMENTS

Social work and counselling

Family Centres

Day care and child-minding services for under fives and school age children

Short-term accommodation (respite care)

Long-term accommodation

Services from occupational therapist, rehabilitation workers, technical officers or assistants, specialist social workers and provision of aids and adaptations

Information on range of services provided by other agencies

Interpreters, translating and range of services for families and children from minority ethnic groups

Advocacy and representation for children and parents

Help with transport costs to visit children living away from home and the provision of cash grants for specific needs which cannot be met in other ways

Holiday play schemes for older children

Toy libraries

Support groups for mothers with young children (not necessarily with a disability)

Home Care services

Home Help service

Rehabilitation services

Loans of equipment, play materials etc. (For natural and foster parents)

Welfare benefits advice

After Care

Adult services

LOCAL EDUCATION AUTHORITIES

Peripatetic services such as home liaison teachers/Portage schemes

Out of school facilities such as after school clubs, holiday play schemes

Advice on residential placements with education

Grants

Adult education (for parents, foster families, care staff etc)

Art, music, sporting and other activities

Careers service

DISTRICT HEALTH AUTHORITIES

Primary and secondary health care including treatment of acute illness

Child health surveillance and rehabilitative services

Child and Adolescent Psychiatric services

Access to child development, district handicap or learning disabilities team

Services of Child Development Centre (which may include playgroup or daycare)

Advice on management of health related problems in other service settings

Support from home visiting services such as community nurses or health visitors

Physiotherapy, occupational therapy and speech therapy provision

Wheelchairs, artificial limbs and mobility aids provision

Health education

Home loans service of medical nursing equipment

Respite and daycare

Counselling and advice on health related issues for parents and children

HOUSING AUTHORITIES

Provision of housing and adaptations

Housing for young people formerly looked after by the local authority

VOLUNTARY ORGANISATIONS

Parent support groups, practical advice and counselling

Daycare (such as play groups, after school clubs and holiday play-schemes)

Volunteer home visitors and home visiting services

Toy Libraries

Adventure Playgrounds and special leisure opportunities for people with disabilities

Respite Care

Residential Care

Education

General advice and support on range of family issues such as financial or welfare problems, housing, racism etc

Advocacy – on an individual and group basis

Interpreters, translating and range of services for families and children from minority ethnic groups

LIBRARY AND INFORMATION SERVICES

Collating and publicising information on range of services for children with special needs. Translation of information material

TRANSPORT AND PLANNING AUTHORITIES

Transport for children in need to services provided by a range of agencies

Road safety education

The design of safe play areas, road schemes, whether local authority, voluntary or run through a private service

THE PRIVATE SECTOR

Independent agencies may provide a wide range of services such as daycare and private nurseries or nursery schools. Some independent agencies provide domiciliary services arrangements on an individual basis. If other local families are using independent provision such as workplace nurseries or private daycare, children with disabilities may benefit from access to a similar service

Residential services (including schools)

THE CHRONICALLY SICK AND DISABLED PERSONS ACT 1970

This Act imposes various duties upon local authorities towards disabled people of all ages, including disabled children as defined in Section 17(11) of the Children Act.

The relevant sections are:

Section 1

As amended by Section 9 of the Disabled Persons Act 1986, this section requires authorities to identify the numbers of disabled people in their area, to publish information about social services provided under Section 2, and to ensure that anyone using a social service is told about any other relevant service available. (See also Schedule 2 paragraph 1 of the Children Act).

Section 2

This section requires authorities to make arrangements for the provision of a number of social services, if they are satisfied that it is necessary for them to do so in order to meet the disabled person's needs. The services which are to be provided as needed are:

- practical assistance in the home;
- provision, or assistance in obtaining radio, television, library or similar recreational facilities;
- lectures, games, outings or other recreational facilities outside the home, or assistance in taking advantage of educational facilities available;
- facilities for, or assistance in, travelling to and from home for various purposes;
- assistance in arranging adaptations to the home, or the provision of additional facilities designed to secure greater safety, comfort or convenience;
- facilitating the taking of holidays;
- meals, whether at home or elsewhere;
- provision, or assistance in obtaining, a telephone and any special equipment needed to enable the disabled person to use it.

Authorities are responsible for making decisions as to entitlement to these services. Once need has been established, provision of the service should be made within a reasonable time.

THE DISABLED PERSONS (SERVICES, CONSULTATION AND REPRESENTATION) ACT 1986

This Act supplements the provisions of the Chronically Sick and Disabled Persons Act 1970 in a number of specific ways, and like the 1970 Act, applies to both disabled children and adults. Some sections have not been implemented as they have effectively been superseded by the community care provisions, including the Children Act.

The main sections in force are as follows:

Section 4

Requires authorities to assess need for services under Section 2 of the 1970 Act.

Sections 5 and 6

Require authorities to identify disabled school leavers and assess their needs for social services.

Requires authorities to take the abilities of carers to continue to provide regular care into consideration when deciding on the need for services.

Section 9

Amends Section 1 of the 1970 Act to require authorities to provide more information.

Section 10

Requires authorities to consult with appropriate organisations of disabled people when making appointments or co-options to any council, committee, or body, of people with special knowledge of the needs of disabled people. It is therefore particularly relevant to local authority social services committees.

THE EDUCATION ACT 1944

This Act places a general duty on local education authorities to provide educational provision for all children of statutory school age including those with special educational needs.

THE EDUCATION ACT 1981

The Act specifies the procedures to be followed by local education authorities when undertaking the assessment and statementing of children with special educational needs (SEN). The Act also contains procedures to be adopted for parental appeals, the approval of independent schools to cater for children with statements of SEN, and the placement of children with statements of SEN at independent schools not approved under the Act.

The Education (Approval of Special Schools) Regulations 1983 and the Education (Approval of Special Schools) (Amendment) Regulations 1991.

The Acts set the standards to be met by maintained and non-maintained special schools.

EDUCATION REFORM ACT 1988

Local education authorities are obliged under section 8 of the 1944 Education Act – as substituted by section 120(6) of the 1988 Education Reform Act – to provide suitable secondary education for all pupils, including those with special educational needs. This provision may be in a college of further education or a school. Although a statement need no longer be maintained for a student at an FE college, the LEA is not released from its duty under section 8 of the 1944 Act to provide for all pupils' education offering such variety of instruction and training as may be desirable in view of their different ages, abilities and aptitudes. The duty of an LEA as described in section 41 of the 1944 Act, as substituted by section 120(2) of the 1988 Education Reform Act, is "to secure the provision for their area of adequate facilities for further education". Sub-section (10) expressly requires LEAs, in fulfilling that duty, also "to have regard to the requirements of persons over compulsory school age who have learning difficulties".

The Act requires all maintained schools, including special schools, to provide the National Curriculum. For a child with a statement, there is no necessity to modify or exempt the requirements of the National Curriculum, but the mechanism exists if modification is in the child's best interests. If a modification is made, a concise definition of the alternative curriculum is required. Inclusion rather than exclusion of pupils with special educational needs in the National Curriculum is being encouraged.

THE EDUCATION (MANDATORY AWARDS) REGULATIONS 1991:

Disabled students allowances: Schedule 2: Part 2, paragraph 12

THE EDUCATION (SPECIAL EDUCATIONAL NEEDS) (APPROVAL OF INDEPENDENT SCHOOLS) REGULATIONS 1991

The Act sets the standards to be met by independent schools wishing to be approved under the Education Act 1981 to cater for children with statements of special educational needs.

THE LOCAL GOVERNMENT AND HOUSING ACT 1989

Disabled Facilities Grant

Under section 114 of the Local Government and Housing Act 1989 local housing authorities are able to give disabled facilities grants to disabled people, including disabled children, to help with the cost of adaptations to enable them to live as independently as possible in their own homes.

The main underlying principle is that disabled people should be able to enjoy comparable facilities in their homes to those enjoyed by able-bodied people. The grant is therefore designed to address the adaptation needs to which a person's disability gives rise by providing:

1. *mandatory grant* for adaptation works of an essential nature.

2. *discretionary grant* for a wide range of works which go beyond basic housing requirements.

The purposes for which mandatory disabled facilities grant can be given are:

– facilitating access to and from the dwelling;

– facilitating access to living rooms, bedrooms and bathroom in the dwelling and facilitating use of facilities in a bathroom;

– facilitating preparation and cooking of food by a disabled person;

– improving the heating system in dwelling and facilitating use by a disabled person of control over sources of power, heat or light;

– facilitating access and movement around dwelling so a disabled person can care for dependent(s) normally resident in dwelling.

Discretionary disabled facilities grant can be given to make a dwelling suitable for the accommodation, welfare or employment of a disabled person eg providing a 'safe' play area for a child.

A local authority is only able to approve a disabled facilities grant where it is satisfied that the works are suitable to meeting the disabled persons adaptation needs. The amount of grant awarded is subject to a test of the applicants financial resources and those of each other 'relevant person' (eg owner or tenant) associated with the application. Housing authorities must consult welfare authorities on whether the works for which grant is sought are 'necessary and appropriate' to meet needs of a disabled person or child. The local authority must decide if it is 'reasonable and practicable' to carry them out in a particular dwelling. If it is impracticable other options (eg rehousing) may need to be explored.

SOCIAL SECURITY BENEFITS

1. There is a wide range of benefits available in respect of children, including those with disabilities. Entitlement to these benefits is dependent on the individual circumstances of the child and his or her family. Some benefits have additions payable if the beneficiary is responsible for a child or children (for example Family Credit, Invalidity Benefit, Severe Disablement Allowance, Disability Working Allowance) and others are only payable if the beneficiary is responsible for children aged under 19 and in full-time education (for example Child Benefit, Widowed Mother's Allowance).

2. The following is a list of benefits payable either to a disabled child, or to the parent or guardian of a disabled child.

i. Benefits payable to a disabled child or young person

These benefits are normally paid direct to the parent or guardian of a child aged under 16.

Extra cost benefits:

Attendance Allowance: A tax-free weekly benefit for a child who has needed a lot of looking after because they are severely disabled, physically or mentally. There are two rates – a lower one for people who need a lot of looking after by day or night, and a higher one for people who need looking after by day and night. For more information see leaflet DS2.

Mobility Allowance: A tax-free cash benefit for a child who is five or older who is unable, or virtually unable, to walk, or who because of both blindness and deafness needs someone with them when they go out of doors. For more information see leaflet NI 211.

Disability Living Allowance: From April 1992, a new benefit replacing Attendance Allowance for people disabled before the age of 65 and Mobility Allowance will be introduced, which will include a new lower rate for less severely disabled people. The qualifying conditions would otherwise be similar to the existing conditions for AA and Mob A. This benefit will have new methods of claiming, assessment and adjudication, with the emphasis placed on the claimant's own assessment of how their illness or disability affects their everyday life. Claimants will need to ask a professional person (eg a GP, health visitor, social worker, community care nurse, occupational therapist etc) involved in their care to corroborate their evidence.

Severe Disablement Allowance: A tax-free benefit for a child aged 16 or over who has been incapable of work for at least 28 weeks because of illness or disablement. For more information see leaflet NI 252.

Income related benefits:

Income Support: Payable only to 16 and 17 year olds who fall within a special group. For example, those who have no choice but to live away from home, or those who are lone parents looking after their child, or those who are incapable of work because they are disabled, or those registered as blind may be able to get Income Support. For more information see leaflet IS 26.

Housing Benefit: A tax-free benefit. Householders on low incomes who find it hard to pay their full rent may be able to get help from their local council, whether or not they are working. For more information see leaflet RR1.

Disability Premium: Payable as part of Income Support and Housing Benefit.

Extra cost benefits:

Invalid Care Allowance: A weekly cash benefit for people of working age who spend a lot of time looking after someone who is getting Attendance Allowance. For more information see leaflet NI 212.

Income related benefits:

Income Support: For people aged 18 or over whose income is below a certain level. To get it they must be available for work and show that they are taking reasonable steps to find a job unless they come under certain categories, such as people who are sick, lone parents and people aged 60 or over. For more information see leaflet IS 1.

Housing Benefit: A tax-free benefit paid by local councils to people on low incomes who find it difficult to pay their full rent. For more information see leaflet RR1.

Community Charge Benefit: A tax-free benefit paid by local councils to people on low incomes who find it difficult to pay their full Community Charge. For more information see leaflet CCB1.

Disabled Child Premium: Payable to people who are in receipt of Income Support, Housing Benefit and/or Community Charge Benefit who are responsible for at least one disabled child.

Social Fund: People on IS who are responsible for disabled children may be entitled to Cold Weather Payments and Community Care Grants. They may also be able to get a Budgeting Loan or a Crisis Loan. For more information see leaflets SB16 and CWP1.

Vaccine Damage Payments: A tax-free lump sum payment for people who have become severely disabled as a result of specified vaccination. For more informaton see leaflet HB3 obtainable from:

Vaccine Damage Payments Unit
DSS
North Fylde Central Office
Norcross
Blackpool
FY5 3TA

Help with NHS Costs: The families of people on IS and Family Credit get help with a range of NHS costs. For more information see leaflet AB11.

Free Milk for Disabled Children: Disabled children between 5 and 16 who are so disabled that they cannot go to school can get free tokens for seven pints of milk a week. For more information see leaflet AB11.

3. If you want more advice about benefits for people with disabilities, contact the Benefit Enquiry Line, a free advice service for people with disabilities, between 9.00 am and 4.30 pm on freephone 0800 882200.

4. If you want to know more about the benefits and how to claim them, you can get the leaflets mentioned here from a Social Security office, or from:

Leaflets Unit
PO Box 21
Stanmore
Middlesex
HA7 1AY

A. DEPARTMENT OF HEALTH (DH) GUIDANCE AND REPORTS RELATING TO THE CHILDREN ACT

DH (1989), *The Care of Children: Principles and Practice in Regulations and Guidance*, HMSO

DH (1989), *An Introduction to the Children Act*, HMSO

DH (1989), *The Children Act 1989 Guidance and Regulations, Volume 1, Court Orders*, HMSO

DH (1991), *The Children Act 1989 Guidance and Regulations, Volume 2, Family Support, Day Care and Educational Provision for Young Children*, HMSO

DH (1991), *The Children Act 1989 Guidance and Regulations, Volume 3, Family Placements*, HMSO

DH (1991), *The Children Act 1989 Guidance and Regulations, Volume 4, Residential Care*, HMSO

DH (1991), *The Children Act 1989 Guidance and Regulations, Volume 5, Independent Schools*, HMSO

DH (1991), *Working Together – A guide to arrangements for inter-agency cooperation for the protection of children from abuse* (second edition)

DH (1991), *Patterns and Outcomes in Child Placement: Messages from Current Research and their Implications*, HMSO

Robbins, D (1990), *Child Care Policy: Putting it in Writing. A Review of English Local Authorities Child Care Policy Statements*, SSI/HMSO

Moss, P and Melhuish, E (1991), *Current Issues in Day Care for Young Children*, Department of Health/Thomas Coram Research Unit, HMSO

Shaw, M, Masson, J, Brocklesby, E (1990), *Children in Need and their Families: a New Approach. A Guide to Part III of the Children Act 1989 for Local Authority Councillors*, University of Leicester School of Social Work and Faculty of Law and the Department of Health

B. ADDITIONAL PUBLICATIONS RELATING TO THE CHILDREN ACT

Adcock, M, White, R, and Hollows, A (1991), *Child Protection: A Training and Practice Resource Pack for Work under the Children Act 1989*, National Children's Bureau

Early Childhood Unit (1991), *Ensuring Standards in the Care of Young Children: Registering and Developing Quality Day Care*, National Children's Bureau

Early Childhood Unit (1991), *Young Children in Group Day Care: Guidelines for Good Practice*, National Children's Bureau

Lyon, C (1991), *The Implications of the Children Act 1989 on Children and Young People with Severe Learning Difficulties*, Barnardos

National Children's Bureau (1990), *Working with the Children Act 1989: Guidelines for Good Practice*, National Children's Bureau

National Children's Bureau (1991), *Residential Care and the Children Act 1989: A Pack for Residential Childcare Staff in Statutory, Voluntary and Private Children's Homes*, National Children's Bureau

C. SOME GENERAL REFERENCES TO PUBLICATIONS FROM GOVERNMENT DEPARTMENTS OR RELATED AGENCIES

Audit Commission (1986), *Making of Community Care*, HMSO

Department of Health (1990), *Caring for People: Community Care in the Next Decade and Beyond*, HMSO

Department of Health (1991), *The Health of the Nation*, HMSO

Department of Health (1988), *Information Needs of Disabled People, their Carers and Service Providers, Final Report*, Department of Health/Coopers and Lybrand

House of Commons Social Services Committee (1990), *Eleventh Report: Services for People with a Mental Handicap*, HMSO

Office of Population and Census Surveys (1989), OPCS Surveys of Disability in Great Britain, HMSO
> *Report 3*: Prevalence of Disability Among Children
> *Report 5*: Financial Circumstances of Families
> *Report 6*: Disabled Children, Services, Transport and Education

Welsh Office – Social Services Inspectorate (1989), Still a Small Voice: Consumer Involvement in the All Wales Strategy, A Survey of Local Authority Perspectives, Welsh Office

Welsh Office (1990), *Review of the All Wales Strategy: Issues for Concern*, Welsh Office

D. SERVICES FOR CHILDREN AND YOUNG PEOPLE WITH DISABILITIES AND THEIR FAMILIES

Baldwin, S (1985), *The Costs of Caring*, Routledge and Kegan Paul

Barnardos (1984), *Carraigfoyle Paediatric Support Unit: The First Two Years*, Barnardos, Irish Division

Brimblecombe, F S W and Russell, P (1987), *Honeylands: Developing a Service for Families with Handicapped Children*, National Children's Bureau

Cameron, J and Sturge-Moore, L (1990), *Ordinary Everyday Families: Action for Families and their Young Children with Special Needs, Disabilities*, MENCAP London Division

Cooke, K and Bradshaw, J (1986), Child Disablement, Family Dissolution and Reconstitution, *Development Medicine and Child Neurology*, Vol 28, 610–18

Cunningham, C and Davis, H (1985), Early Parent Counselling, in Craft, M, Bicknell, J and Hollings, S, ed *Mental Handicap: A Multidisciplinary Approach*, Balliere Tindall

Cunningham, C and Davis, H (1985), *Working with Parents: Frameworks for Collaboration*, Open University Press

Department of Health/Social Services Inspectorate (1984), *Local Authority Social Services for Handicapped Children in England*, Department of Health

Gath, A (1978), *Down's Syndrome and the Family*, Academic Press

Glendinning, C (1983), *Unshared Care–Parents and their Disabled Children*, Routledge and Kegan Paul

Glendinning, C, (1986), *A Single Door: Social Work with Families of Disabled Children*, Allen and Unwin

Gregory, S (1976), *The Deaf Child and His Family*, Allen and Unwin

Hatch, S and Hinton, T (1987), *Self Help in Practice: A Study of Contact a Family in Wandsworth*, Community Care/Social Work Monographs

Hewitt, S, Newson, E and Newson, J (1970), *The Family and the Handicapped Child*, George Allen and Unwin

Howlin, P and Rutter, M, (1989), *Treatment of Autistic Children*, John Wiley

Kew, S (1975), *Handicap and Family Crisis*, Pitman

Kornblatt, E and Heinrich, J (1985), *Needs and Coping Abilities in Families of Children with Developmental Disabilities, Mental Retardation*, 29, 1, 13–19

Lawton, D and Quine, L (1989), *Patterns of Take-up of the Family Fund: the Characteristics of Eligible Non-Claimants and the Reasons for Not Claiming*, Family Fund/Child: Health and Development

McConachie, H (1986), *Parents and Young Mentally Handicapped Children: A Review of Research Issues*, Croom Helm

Mittler, P and McConachie, H (1983), *Parents, Professionals and Mentally Handicapped People: Approaches to Partnership*, Croom Helm

Pahl, J and Quine, E (1984), *Families with Mentally Handicapped Children, A Study of Stress and a Service Response*, Health Services Research Unit, University of Kent

Pahl, J and Quine, E (1987), Families with Mentally Handicapped Children in Orford, ed, *Coping with Disorder in the Family*, Croom Helm

Pugh, G (1981), *Parents as Partners*, National Children's Bureau

Quine, L and Pahl, J (1985), Examining the Cause of Stress in Families with Severely Mentally Handicapped Children, in *British Journal of Social Work*, 15, 501–517

Quine, L and Pahl, J (1989), *Stress and Coping in Families Caring for a Child with Severe Mental Handicap: A Longitudinal Study*, Institute of Social and Applied Psychology and Centre for Health Services Studies

Van der Eyken, W (1982), *Home-Start: A Four Year Evaluation*, Home-Start Consultancy, Leicester

Wilkin, D (1979), *Caring for the Mentally Handicapped Child*, Croom Helm

Wolkind, S (1981), Depression in Mothers of Young Children, *Archives of Disease in Childhood*, Vol 56, NO 1, 1–3

E. SPECIAL EDUCATIONAL NEEDS

Cameron, R J (1986), *Portage: Ten Years of Achievement*, NFER/Nelson

Clarke, M (1988), *Children under Five: Educational Research and Evidence*, Gordon Breach Scientific Publishers

Department of Education and Science (1978), *Report of Committee of Enquiry into Special Educational Needs* (Warnock Report), HMSO

Department of Education and Science (1989), *Assessments and Statements of Special Educational Needs: Procedures within the Education, Health and Social Services*, Circular 22/89

Fish, J (Chair), (1985), *Equal Opportunities for all? Report of the Committee Reviewing Provision to Meet Special Educational Needs*, ILEA/London

Goacher, B, Evans, J, Welton, J, Wedell, K (1988), *Policy and Provision for Special Educational Needs: Implementing the 1981 Education Act*, Cassell

Hedderley, R and Jennings, K (1987), *Extending and Developing Portage*, NFER/Nelson

House of Commons Education, Science and Arts Committee (1989), *Report of Enquiry into Nursery Education*, HMSO

House of Commons Education, Science and Arts Committee (1987), *Report of Enquiry into the Implementation of the 1981 Education Act*, HMSO

McConkey, R (1985), *Working with Parents: A Practical Guide for Teachers and Therapists*, Croom Helm

Mittler, P and Mittle, H (1986), *Parents as Partners*, National Council for Special Education

National Curriculum Council (1989), *A Curriculum for All*, Report of the Task Group *on Special Educational Needs*, National Curriculum Council, York

Pugh, G (1987), *Services for Under-Fives: Developing a Coordinated Approach*, National Children's Bureau

Sylva, K (1986), *Monitoring the High Scope Training Programme 1984–5*, University of Oxford, Department of Social and Administrative Studies

Wedell, K and Welton, J (1988), *Children with Special Educational Needs: A Source Book of Information, Ideas and Discussion Points*, the 1981 Education Act Management Development Project, Institute of Education, University of London

Wolfendale, S (ed) (1989), *Parental Involvement: Developing Networks Between School, Home and Community*, Cassell

Wolfendale, S (1988), *The Parental Contribution to Assessment*, Developing Horizons No 10, National Council for Special Education

Wolfendale, S (1983), *Parental Participation in Children's Development and Education*, Gordon Breach

F. CHILD HEALTH

Department of Health (1991), *Welfare of Children and Young People in Hospital*, HSG(91)1, HMSO

Department of Health (1976), *Fit for the Future – Report of the Court Committee on Child Health Services*, HMSO

NAWCH (1990), *The NAWCH Quality Review – Setting Standards for Children in Health Care*, National Association for the Welfare of Children in Hospital

Graham, P, Kurtz, Z, ed. (1987), *Investing in the Future – Child Health Ten Years After the Court Report*, National Children's Bureau

British Paediatric Association (1985), *Working Party on the Needs and Care of Adolescents*, BPA, London

British Paediatric Association (1990), *The Integration of Child Health Services*, BPA, London

Elfer, P and Gatiss, S (1990), *Charting Child Health Services: A Survey of Community Child Health Services Provided by Health Authorities in England, Scotland and Wales*, National Children's Bureau

Butler, J (1989), *Child Health Surveillance in Primary Care – A Critical Review*, HMSO

Department of Health (1989), *Working for Patients*, HMSO

Department of Health (1991), *The Health of the Nation*, HMSO

Hall, D (1989), *Health for All Children – A Programme for Child Health Surveillance*, Oxford Medical Publications

Hochstadt, N and Yost, D (1991), *The Medically Complex Child: The Transition to Home Care*, Harwood Academic Publishers, London and New York

Hogg, C and Rodin, J (1989), *Quality Review*, National Association for the Welfare of Children in Hospital

Barker, W and Anderson, R (1988), *The Child Development Programme – An Evaluation of Process and Outcome*, University of Bristol

G. CARE OF CHILDREN WITH LIFE-THREATENING OR TERMINAL CONDITIONS

Baum, J, Frances Dominica, Sister, Woodward, R (1990), *Listen: My Child has a Lot of Living to Do: Caring for Children with Life-Threatening Conditions*, Oxford University Press

Dominica, F, Sister (1987), The Role of the Hospice for the Dying Child, *British Journal of Hospital Medicine*, 38, 334–43

National Association of Health Authorities and Trusts (1987), *Caring of the Dying: A Guide for Health Authorities*, Report of Working Party, King Edward's Hospital Fund for London/National Association of Health Authorities, Birmingham

National Association of Health Authorities and Trusts (1988), *Care of Dying Children and their Families*, Report of Working Party, National Association of Health Authorities, Birmingham

Salvage, J (1986), *Hospices for Children: A Need in a Sick Society?* Proceedings of a Conference organised jointly by King's Fund Centre and Helen House Hospice, King's Fund Paper 86/181, King's Fund

H. RESPITE CARE

Banks, S, and Grizzell, E (1984), *A Study of Family Placement for the Shared Care of Handicapped Children in Norfolk and Oxfordshire*, SSI/DOH

Fenwick, J (1986), *Respite Family Care and Mental Handicap in Newcastle*, City of Newcastle Policy Services and Social Services Department

Hill, M (1987), *Sharing Childcare in Early Parenthood*, Kegan Paul

Hubert, J (1991), *Home-Bound: Crisis in the Care of Young People with Severe Learning Difficulties*, King's Fund Centre

Orlick, C, Robinson, C and Russell, O (1991), *A Survey of Family Based Respite Care Schemes in the United Kingdom*, Norah Fry Research Centre, Bristol

Oswin, M (1984), *They Keep Going Away*, King Edward Hospital Fund/ Blackwells

Robinson, C (1986), *Avon Short Term Respite Care Scheme: Evaluation Study*, Final Report, Department of Mental Health, University of Bristol

Robinson, C and Stalker, K (1989), *Time for a Break.* An Interim Report to the Department of Health, Norah Fry Research Centre, University of Bristol

Social Services Inspectorate (NW Division) (1989), *Care for a Change? Inspection of Short Term Care in the Personal Social Services*, SSI, Manchester

Stalker, K (1990), *Share the Care: An Evaluation of a Family Based Respite Care Service*, Jessica Kingsley Publishers

Stalker, K and Robinson, C (1991), *You're on the Waiting List: Families Waiting for Respite Care*, Fourth Interim Report, Norah Fry Research Centre, University of Bristol

Stalker, K and Robinson, C (1991), *Out of Touch – The Non-Users of Respite Care Services*, Norah Fry Research Centre, University of Bristol

Taylor, R (1984), *Share the Care: Summary and Assessment*, Unpublished Report to Lothian Regional Social Work Committee

I. CHILDREN LIVING AWAY FROM HOME

Aldgate, J (1990), Foster Children at School: Success or Failure, *Adoption and Fostering*, Vol 14, No 4

Aldgate, J (1990), *Using Written Agreements with Children and Families*, Family Rights Group, London

Atkinson, D (1988), Residential Care for Children and Adults with Mental Handicap, in *Residential Care: The Research Reviewed*, National Institute of Social Work/HMSO

Bamford, F N and Wolkind, S N, (1988), *The Physical and Mental Health of Children in Care: Research Needs*, ESRC

Berridge, D and Cleaver, H (1987), *Foster Home Breakdown*, Blackwells

Cliffe, D (1990), *An End to Residential Care? The Warwickshire Direction*, National Children's Bureau

Jackson, S (1987), *The Education of Children in Care*, Bristol Papers in Applied Social Studies, No 1, the School of Applied Social Studies, University of Bristol

Kahan, B (1989), The Physical and Mental Health of Children in Care, in Kahan, B (ed), *Child Care Research: Policy and Practice*, Open University/ Hodder and Stoughton

Leonard, A (1991), *Homes of their Own: A Community Care Initiative for Children with Learning Difficulties*, Gower Publishing Group

Levy, A and Kahan, B (1991), *The Pindown Experience and the Protection of Children*, Staffordshire County Council

Lyon, C (1990), *Living Away From Home: The Legal Impact on Young People with Severe Learning Difficulties*, Barnados NW Division

Milham, S, Bullock, R, Hosie, K and Little, M (1986), *Lost in Care: The Problems of Maintaining Links between Children in Care and their Families*, Gower Publishing Group

Sinclair, R (To be published Winter 1991), *Residential Care and the Children Act 1989: A Pack for Residential Child Care Staff in Statutory, Voluntary and Private Children's Homes*, National Children's Bureau

Ong, B and Alazewski, A (1988), *Study of Barnardo's Croxteth Park Project*, University of Hull

Shearer, A (1980), *Handicapped Children in Residential Care: A Study of Policy Failure*, Bedford Square Press

Sinclair, I (ed) (1988), *Residential Care: The Research Reviewed*, Vol 2, Wagner Report, HMSO/London

Thoburn, J, Murdoch, A and O'Brien, A (1986), *Permanence in Child-Care*, Blackwell

Triseliotis, J and Russell, J (1984), *Hard to Place: The Outcomes of Adoption and Residential Care*, ESRC/DOH Studies in Deprivation and Disadvantage, Heineman Educational Books

Utting, J (1991), *Children in Public Care*, Department of Health/HMSO

J. CHILDREN WITH DISABILITIES AND SPECIAL NEEDS FROM MINORITY ETHNIC GROUPS

Bahl, V (1987), *The Asian Mother and Baby Campaign*, Department of Health

Baxter, C, Poonia, K, Ward, L and Nadirshaw, Z (1990), *Double Discrimination: Issues and Services for People with Learning Difficulties from Black and Ethnic Minority Communities*, King's Fund Centre/Commission for Racial Equality

Black, J A (1991), The Medical Needs of Ethnic Minority Children in Britain, *Current Paediatrics*, 1, 53–8, Longman Group UK

Contact a Family (1989), *Reaching Black Families? A Study of Contact a Family in Lewisham and the Relevance of Services for Black Families who have Children with Disabilities and Special Needs*, Contact a Family

Contact a Family (1989), *The Educational Needs of Ethnic Minority Children Who Have Disabilities and Special Needs*, Contact a Family/Ealing Race Equality Unit

Davis, H and Russell, P (1989), *Physical and Mental Handicap in the Asian Community – Can My Child Be Helped?* National Children's Bureau

MacDonald, S (1991), *All Equal Under the Act? A Practical Guide to the Children Act 1989 for Social Workers*, Race Equality Unit

Nathwani, A and Perkins, N (1987), *Disability and Ethnic Minority Communities – A Study in Three London Boroughs*, Greater London Association for Disabled People

Osborn, A F and Butler, N R (1985), *Ethnic Minority Children. A Comparative Study from Birth to Five Years*, Report of the Child Health and Education Commission for Racial Equality

K. TRANSITION TO ADULT SERVICES – YOUNG PEOPLE WITH DISABILITIES

Beardshaw, V and Towell, D (1990), *Assessment and Case Management: Implications for the Implementation of Caring for People*, King's Fund Institute

Brimblecombe, F S W (1985), *The Needs of Handicapped Young Adults*, Department of Child Health, University of Exeter

British Paediatric Association and British Paediatric Neurologists' Association Joint Working Party (1986), *Adolescence and Disability*, BPA

Griffiths, M (1989), *Enabled to Work? Support into Employment for Young People with Disabilities*, Further Education Unit

Cooper, D (1989), *Education and Training: An Introduction to Some Training Opportunities for Young People with Disabilities in the UK*, FEU

Hirst, M (1985), Dependency and Family Care of Young Adults with Disabilities, *Child Care Health and Development*, 11, 241–257

Hirst, M (1987), Carers of Young People with Disabilities between ages 15 and 21 Years, *Disability, Handicap and Society*, 2, 1

Hirst, M (1985), Young Adults with Disabilities: Health, Employment and Financial Costs for Family Carers, *Child Care Health and Development*, 11, 291–307

Hunter, D J (ed) (1988), *Bridging the Gap: Case Management and Advocacy for People with Physical Handicaps*, King Edward's Hospital Fund for London

Prince of Wales Advisory Group (1984), *Independent Living Options*, Prince of Wales Advisory Group/London

Richardson A and Ritchie, J (1986), *Making the Break*, King's Fund

Royal Association for Disability and Rehabilitation (1990), *From Passivity to Empowerment*, RADAR

Towell, D, (ed) (1988), *An Ordinary Life in Practice: Developing Comprehensive Community-Based Services for People with Learning Disabilities*, King Edward's Hospital Fund for London

Towell, D and Beardshaw, V (1991), *Enabling Community Integration: The Role of Public Authorities in Promoting an Ordinary Life for People with Learning Disabilities in the 1990s*, King's Fund College

Warburton, R W (1990), *Developing Services for Disabled People: Results of An Inspection to Monitor the Operation of the Disabled Persons Act*, SSI/Department of Health

Wertheimer, A (1989), *Self-Advocacy and Parents: Self-Advocacy and Its Impact on the Parents of Young People with Disabilities*, FEU

This Glossary is reproduced by the kind permission of the Open University.

It is intended to provide relatively simple explanations of the most important terms and phrases used. There are basically three kinds of entry. First, we have included phrases given a specific meaning within the Children Act 1989 (such as 'accommodation'). These are intended to be generally useful to aid familiarisation with the new terminology. Where appropriate we have added cross-references to the Act itself; where we quote directly from the Act we use quotation marks. Secondly, we have included some legal terms which may be unfamiliar to non-lawyers (such as 'affidavit'), in order to make the legal terminology more comprehensible. Finally, we have included terms which have specific meanings in child care work (such as 'assessment'), to clarify what these mean in the context in which we have used them. We have tried to be as comprehensive as practicable, without overburdening our text. You may wish to add to the Glossary yourself, to make it more suited to your needs.

Accommodation: being provided with accommodation replaces the old voluntary care concept. It refers to a service that the local authority provides to the parents of children in need, and their children. The child is not in care when s/he is being provided with accommodation; nevertheless the local authority has a number of duties towards children for whom it is providing accommodation, including the duty to discover the child's wishes regarding the provision of accommodation and to give them proper consideration. [s.20]

Adoption: the total transfer of parental responsibility from the child's natural parents to the adopter/s.

Affidavit: a statement in writing and on oath sworn before a person who has the authority to administer it, eg a solicitor.

Appeal: an appeal in care proceedings will now be heard by the High Court or, where applicable, the Court of Appeal. All parties to the proceedings will have equal rights of appeal. On hearing an appeal, the High Court can make such orders as may be necessary to give effect to its decision. [s.94]

Area Child Protection Committee [ACPC]: based upon the boundaries of the local authority, it provides a forum for developing, monitoring and reviewing the local child protection policies, and promoting effective and harmonious co-operation between the various agencies involved. Although there is some variation from area to area, each committee is made up of representatives of the key agencies, who have authority to speak and act on their agency's behalf. ACPCs issue guidelines about procedures, tackle significant issues that arise, offer advice about the conduct of cases in general, make policy and review progress on prevention, and oversee inter-agency training.

Assessment: a complex and skilled process of gathering together and evaluating information about a child, his/her family, and their circumstances. Its purpose is to determine children's needs, in order to plan for their immediate and long-term care, and decide what services and resources must be provided. Child care assessments are usually co-ordinated by social services, but depend upon teamwork with other agencies (such as education and health). Detailed information about conducting assessments in child protection cases is provided in Protecting Children: a guide for social workers undertaking a comprehensive assessment (Department of Health, 1987).

Authorised person: in relation to care and supervision proceedings, a person other than the local authority, authorised by the Secretary of State to bring proceedings under s.31 of the Act. This covers the NSPCC and its officers. Elsewhere in the Act there is a reference to persons who are authorised to carry out specified functions, eg to enter and inspect independent schools. You should refer to the sections of the Act and the Regulations for further information on the powers of such authorised persons.

Care order: an order made by the court under s.31(1)(a) of the Act placing the child in the care of the designated local authority. A care order includes an interim care order except where express provision to the contrary is made. [s.31(11)]

Case conference: in a child care context, a formal meeting attended by representatives from all the agencies concerned with the child's welfare. Increasingly this includes the child's parents, and the Act promotes this practice. Its purpose is to gather together and evaluate all the relevant information about a child, and plan any immediate action which may be necessary to protect the child (eg seeking a court order). Where the meeting decides that the child and family need support, a keyworker will be appointed to co-ordinate an inter-agency plan for work with a child and the family, and the child's name (plus those of any other children living in the same household) may be entered on the Child Protection Register.

Child: a person under the age of eighteen. There is an important exception to this in the case of an application for financial relief by a 'child' who has reached eighteen and is, or will be, receiving education or training. [Sched 1, paras 2, 6 and 16]

Child assessment order: an order under s.43 of the Act. The order requires any person who can do so to produce the child for an assessment and to comply with the terms of the order.

Child Protection Register: a central record of all children in a given area for whom support is being provided via inter-agency planning. Generally, these are children considered to be at risk of abuse or neglect. The register is usually maintained and run by social-service departments under the responsibility of a custodian (an experienced social worker able to provide advice to any professional making enquiries about the child). Registration for each child is reviewed every six months.

Childminder: a person who looks after one or more children under the age of eight for reward for more than two hours in any one day. [s.71]

Children in need: a child is 'in need' if:

"(a) he is unlikely to achieve or maintain, or have the opportunity of achieving or maintaining, a reasonable standard of health or development without the provision for him of services by a local authority . . .

(b) his health or development is likely to be significantly impaired or further impaired, without the provision for him of such services; or

(c) he is disabled." [s.17(10)]

Children living away from home: children who are not being looked after by the local authority but are nevertheless living away from home, eg children in independent schools. The local authority has a number of duties towards such children, eg to take reasonably practicable steps to ensure that their welfare is being adequately safeguarded and promoted.

Complaints procedure: the procedure that the local authority must set up to hear representations regarding the provision of services under Part III of the Act from a number of persons, including the child, the parents and 'such other person as the authority consider has sufficient interest in the child's welfare to warrant his representations being considered by them'. [s.26(3)]. This procedure must contain an independent element.

Concurrent jurisdiction: by virtue of s92(7) the High Court, a county court and a magistrates' court (Family Proceedings Court) will have jurisdiction to hear all proceedings under the Act, with some clearly limited exceptions. It is also possible for all proceedings involving the same child and family, irrespective of where they started, to be heard in the same court.

Contact: between a child and another person includes visits, stays, outings and communication by letter and telephone. Under s.34 of the Act the local authority is under a duty to allow a child in care reasonable contact with a number of persons, including the child's parents.

Contact order: an order 'requiring the person with whom a child lives, or is to live, to allow the child to visit or stay with the person named in the order, or for that person and the child otherwise to have contact with each other'. [s.8]

Court welfare officer: an officer appointed to provide a report for the court about the child and the child's family situation and background. The court welfare officer will usually be a probation officer. The court may request either the local authority or the court welfare officer to prepare a report. [s.7(1)]

Day care: a person provides day care if s/he looks after one or more children under the age of eight on non-domestic premises for more than two hours in any day. [s.71] In relation to the local authority provision of day care, it refers to any form of supervised activity provided for children during the day. [s.18(4)]

Development: 'physical, intellectual, emotional, social or behavioural development'. [s.31(9)]

Disabled: a child is disabled if 'he is blind, deaf, or dumb or suffers from mental disorder of any kind or is substantially and permanently handicapped by illness, injury or congenital deformity or such other disability as may be prescribed'. [s.17(11)]

Disclosure interview: a term sometimes used to indicate an interview with a child, conducted as part of the assessment for suspected sexual abuse. It is misleading (since it implies, in some people's view, undue pressure on the child to 'disclose') and therefore the preferred term is 'investigative interview'.

Duty to investigate: the local authority is under a duty to investigate in a number of situations. The general investigative duty arises where the local authority has 'reasonable cause to suspect that a child who lives, or is found, in [its] area is suffering, or is likely to suffer, significant harm'; it must make such enquiries as it considers necessary to enable it to decide whether it should take any action to safeguard or promote the child's welfare. [s.47(1)]

Educational psychologist: a psychology graduate who has had teaching experience and additional vocational training. Educational psychologists perform a range of functions, including assessing children's educational, psychological and emotional needs, offering therapy and contributing psychological expertise to the process of assessment.

Education supervision order: an order under s.36(1) which puts the child under the supervision of a designated local education authority.

Education Welfare Officer (EWO): provides social work support to children in the context of their schooling. While EWO's main focus used to be the enforcement of school attendance, today they perform a wider range of services, including seeking to ensure that children receive adequate and appropriate education and that any special needs are met, and more general liaison between local authority education and social services departments. Their approach is primarily supportive and directed towards children's educational entitlements.

Emergency protection order: an order under s.44 which the court can make if it is satisfied that a child is likely to suffer significant harm, or where enquiries are being made with respect to the child and they are being frustrated by the unreasonable refusal of access to the child. The effect of the order is to operate as a direction to any person in a position to do so to comply with any request to produce the child, and it authorises the removal of the child or the prevention of the child's removal. The order gives the applicant parental responsibility for the child. [s.44]

Evidence: s.96 of the Act allows a child who does not in the opinion of the court understand the nature of an oath to give evidence if the court considers that the child understands that it is his/her duty to speak the truth and that s/he has sufficient understanding to justify the evidence being heard. Sections 7 and 41 permit the inclusion of what would be hearsay evidence (ie evidence of a fact not directly seen or heard by the witness) in reports written by social workers, court welfare officers and GALs.

Family assistance order: an order under s.16 of the Act requiring either a probation officer or a social worker to 'advise, assist and befriend' a named person for a period of six months or less. The named person can be the child's parents, guardian, those with whom the child lived or who had contact with the child, and the child him/herself.

Family Centre: a centre which the child and parents, and any other person looking after the child, can attend for occupational and recreational activities, advice, guidance or counselling, and accommodation while receiving such advice, guidance or counselling. [Sched 2 para 9]

Family Panel: the new panel from which the magistrates who sit in the new Family Proceedings Court are selected. These magistrates will have undergone specialist training on the Act.

Family proceedings: these are defined in s.8(3) as any proceedings under the inherent jurisdiction of the High Court in relation to children; and under parts I, II and IV of the Act, the Matrimonial Causes Act 1973, the Domestic Violence and Matrimonial Proceedings Act 1976, the Adoption Act 1976, the Domestic Proceedings and Magistrates' Courts Act 1978, ss.1 and 9 of the Matrimonial Homes Act 1983, and Part III of the Matrimonial and Family Proceedings Act 1984. Note: proceedings under Part V of the Children Act 1989, ie orders for the protection of children, are not family proceedings.

Family Proceedings Court: the new court at the level of the magistrates' court to hear proceedings under the Children Act 1989. The magistrates will be selected from a new panel, known as the Family Panel, and will be specially trained.

Fieldworker (field social worker): conducts a range of social work functions in the community and in other settings (eg hospitals). Most fieldworkers carry their own case-load, and, following career progression, undertake supervision of others and/or specialise either with a particular group (eg older people) or in a particular function (eg running the home-help service). In many (but by no means all) local authorities specialist social workers have been appointed to co-ordinate child protection work and offer particular expertise (eg in conducting joint investigative interviews with police officers).

Foster-carer: a foster-carer provides substitute family care for children. A child looked after by a local authority can be placed with local authority foster-parent under s.23(2)(a). Under the Act, Part IX regulates the private foster-care of children for more than 27 days. Foster-carers are subject to the usual fostering limit of three children unless they are siblings or the local authority grants them an exemption. Short-term care of children under eight may be subject to the childminding provisions in Part X.

Guardian ad litem (GAL): a person appointed by the court to investigate a child's circumstances and to report to the court. The GAL does not represent the child but seeks to present a non-partisan view of the child's welfare. The GAL can appoint a solicitor for the child. In some cases the Official Solicitor acts as the GAL.

Guidance: local authorities are required to act in accordance with the Guidance issued by the Secretary of State. However, Guidance does not have the full force of law but is intended as a series of statements of good practice and may be quoted or used in court proceedings.

Harm: defined as 'ill-treatment or the impairment of health or development'. [s.31(9)]

Health: physical or mental health.

Ill-treatment: includes sexual abuse and forms of ill-treatment which are not physical.

In care: refers to a child in the care of the local authority by virtue of an order under s.31(1)(a) or an interim order under s.38 of the Act.

Independent visitor: the local authority in certain sets of circumstances appoints such a visitor for a child it is looking after. The visitor appointed has the duty of 'visiting, advising and befriending the child'. [Sched 2, para 17]

Inherent jurisdiction: the powers of the High Court to make orders to protect a child which are not based on statute and which are outside the established wardship jurisdiction.

Injunction: an order made by the court prohibiting an act or requiring its cessation. Under the Domestic Violence and Matrimonial Proceedings Act 1976 the county court has the power to make injunctions. Injunctions can be either interlocutory (ie temporary, pending the outcome of the full hearing) or perpetual.

Inter-agency plan: a plan devised jointly by the agencies concerned in a child's welfare which co-ordinates the services they provide. Its aim is to ensure that the support offered meets all the child's needs, so far as this is practicable, and that duplication and rivalry are avoided. The plan should specify goals to be achieved, resources and services to be provided, the allocation of responsibilities, and arrangements for monitoring and review.

Interim care order: an order made by the court under s.38 placing the child in the care of the designated local authority. There are complex provisions as to its duration, with a special initial period of eight weeks. There is no limit to the number of interim care orders that can be made.

Interim supervision order: see **Interim care order**

Investigative interview: the preferred term for an interview conducted with a child as part of an assessment following concerns that the child may have been abused (most notably, in cases of suspected sexual abuse). In many areas these interviews are conducted jointly by specially trained social workers and police officers, in order to reduce the number of times children are expected to tell their story and for information to be gathered in ways that make it acceptable as evidence, if the need arises.

Judicial review: an order from the divisional court quashing a disputed decision. The divisional court cannot substitute its own decision but can merely send the matter back to the offending authority for reconsideration.

Keyworker: a social worker allocated specific responsibility for a particular child. In residential settings, this will be the person who will maintain an overall interest in the child's welfare, and will often undertake specific work with the child on a day-to-day basis. In a fieldwork child care setting, the keyworker is appointed at a case conference, and is responsible for co-ordinating the work done with and for the child by the different agencies (eg health, education, housing).

Legal aid: available in proceedings under the Act. There is neither a merits nor a means test in relation to proceedings under s.25 relating to secure accommodation.

Looked after: a child is looked after when s/he is in local authority care or is being provided with accommodation by the local authority. [s.22(1)]

Monitoring: where plans for a child, and the child's safety and well-being, are systematically appraised on a routine basis. Its function is to oversee the child's continued welfare and enable any necessary action or change to be instigated speedily, and at a managerial level, to ensure that proper professional standards are being maintained.

Official Solicitor: an officer of the Supreme Court who acts on behalf of children in certain cases. When representing a child the Official Solicitor acts both as a solicitor as well as a guardian ad litem.

Paramountcy principle: the principle that the welfare of the child is the paramount consideration in proceedings concerning children.

Parental responsibility: defined as 'all the rights, duties, powers, responsibilities and authority which by law a parent of a child has in relation to the child and his property'. [s.3(1)] Parental responsibility can be exercised by persons who are not the child's biological parent and can be shared among a number of persons. It can be acquired by agreement or court order.

Parties: parties to proceedings are entitled to attend the hearing, present their case and examine witnesses. The Act envisages that children will automatically be parties in care proceedings. Anyone with parental responsibility for the child will also be a party to such proceedings, as will the local authority. Others may be able to acquire party status. A person with party status will be eligible for legal aid in order to be legally represented at the hearing. If you have party status you are also able to appeal against the decision. Others who are not parties may be entitled to make representations. For further information on this, refer to the Rules of Court.

Permanency planning: deciding on the long-term future of children who have been moved from their families. Its purpose is to ensure them a permanent, stable and secure upbringing, either within their original family or by providing high-quality alternative parenting (for example, living permanently with grandparents or other relatives, or being adopted). Its aim is to avoid long periods of insecurity or repeated disruptions in children's lives. Hence it should be completed speedily, preferably within six months of a child first moving away from home.

Police protection: s.46 allows the police to detain a child or prevent his/her removal for up to 72 hours if they believe that the child would otherwise suffer significant harm. There are clear duties on the police to consult the child, if this is practicable, and to notify various persons of their action, eg the child's parents and the local authority.

Preliminary hearing: a hearing to clarify matters in dispute, to agree evidence, and to give directions as to the timetable of the case and the disclosure of evidence.

Probation officer: a welfare professional employed as an officer of the court and financed jointly by the local authority and the Home Office. In addition to taking on a case-load, most probation officers undertake some specialist work, such as conducting groupwork with offenders or helping to run a phone-in service. An important role is the provision of welfare reports of various kinds.

Prohibited steps order: an order that 'no step which could be taken by a parent in meeting his parental responsibility for a child, and which is of a kind specified in the order, shall be taken by any person without the consent of the court'. [s.8(1)]

Recovery order: an order which the court can make when there is reason to believe that a child who is in care, the subject of an emergency protection order or in police protection has been unlawfully taken or kept away from the responsible person, or has run away or is staying away from the responsible person, or is missing. The effect of the recovery order is to require any person who is in a position to do so to produce the child on request, to authorise the removal of the child by any authorised person, and to require any person who has information as to the child's whereabouts to disclose that information, if asked to do so to a constable or officer of the court. [s.50]

Refuge: s.51 enables 'safe houses' legally to provide care for children who have run away from home or local authority care. However, a recovery order can be obtained in relation to a child who has run away to a refuge.

Regulations: refer to the supplementary powers and duties issued by the Secretary of State under the authority of the Act. These cover a wide range of issues, from secure accommodation to the procedure for considering representations (including complaints), and have the full force of law.

Rehabilitation: in a child care context, the process of working with children and parents, and providing resources and support to enable children to return home to be brought up in their families, for the children's needs to be met, and to help overcome the problems that led to their needing to live away.

Representations: see **Complaints procedure**.

Residence order: an order 'setting the arrangements to be made as to the person with whom a child is to live'. [s.8(1)]

Residential social worker: provides day-to-day care, support and therapy for children living in residential settings, such as children's homes. Until recently most residential social workers were unqualified. As the importance and

demands of their work have become increasingly recognised, more training opportunities are being provided.

Respite care: a service giving family members or other carers short breaks from their caring responsibilities. It is intended to support the care of people (eg those with disabilities or infirmities) in the community who might otherwise need to be placed in full-time residential care.

Responsible person: in relation to a supervised child, 'any person who has parental responsibility for the child, and any other person with whom the child is living'. With their consent the responsible person can be required to comply with certain obligations. [Sched 3, paras 1 and 3]

Review: under s.26 local authorities are under a duty to conduct regular reviews in order to monitor the progress of children they are looking after. When holding reviews local authorities must comply with their duties as given in s.22. Reviews are opportunities to consider progress and any problems and changes in circumstances, and to resolve difficulties, set new goals and plan for the future. They are usually attended by all those with significant responsibilities for the child. The child and his/her parents should also attend, and be given help and support to participate in the decision making and to make sure their views and wishes are known. [s.26]

Rules: Rules of Court produced by the Lord Chancellor's Department and the Home Office. These lay down the procedural rules which govern the operation of the courts under the Children Act 1989.

Section 8 orders: the four new orders contained in the Act which, to varying degrees, regulate the exercise of parental responsibility.

Secure accommodation: s.25 provides for the circumstances in which a child who is being looked after can be placed in secure accommodation. Such accommodation is provided for the purpose of restricting the liberty of the child.

Significant harm: s.31(10) states: 'Where the question of whether harm suffered by the child is significant turns on the child's health or development, his health or development shall be compared with that which could reasonably be expected of a similar child'.

Social worker: a generic term applying to a wide range of staff who undertake different kinds of social welfare responsibilities. These include advising and supporting individuals and families during periods of trouble, both within the community and in residential settings; accessing resources, benefits and services; conducting assessments and investigations and monitoring standards of care. Social workers may be employed by local authorities, courts or voluntary organisations (see **Residential social worker, Fieldworker, Education Welfare Officer** and **Probation officer**).

Specific issue order: an order 'giving directions for the purpose of determining a specific question which has arisen, or which may arise, in connection with any aspect of parental responsibility for a child'. [s.8(1)]

Supervision order: an order under s.31(1)(b) and including, except where express contrary provision is made, an interim supervision order under s.38. [s.31]

Supervisor: the person under whose supervision the child is placed by virtue of an order under ss.31 and 38. The powers and duties of the supervisor are contained in s.35 and Sched 3.

Timetables: under the Act the court, pursuant to the principle of avoiding delay because it is harmful for the child, has the power to draw up a timetable and give directions for the conduct of the case in any proceedings in which the making of a Section 8 order arises, and in applications for care and supervision orders. [ss.11 and 32]

Transitional arrangements: the arrangements relating to children who are the subjects of existing orders under legislation prior to the implementation of the Children Act 1989. The general rule is that where this is the case, the child will be treated as if s/he were the subject of the nearest equivalent order in the Act.

Ward of court: a child who as the subject of wardship proceedings, is under the protection of the High Court. No important decision can be taken regarding the child while s/he is a ward of court without the consent of the wardship court.

Wardship: the legal process whereby control is exercised over the child in order to protect the child and safeguard his/her welfare.

Welfare checklist: refers to the innovatory checklist contained in s.1(3) of the Act. This checklist applies in all contested Section 8 proceedings and all proceedings under Part IV of the Act. It does not apply in proceedings under Part V of the Act on child protection.

Welfare report: s.7 of the Act gives the court the power to request a report on any question in respect of child under the Act. The report can be presented by either a probation officer or an officer of the local authority. Section 7(4) provides that regardless of any rule of law to the contrary, the court may take account of any statement contained in the report and any evidence given in respect of matters referred to in the report as long as the court considers them relevant.

Written agreement: the agreement arrived at between the local authority and the parents of children for whom it is providing services. These arrangements are part of the partnership model that is seen as good practice under the Act.

Printed in the United Kingdom for HMSO
Dd301682 11/95 C20 G3397 10170